PRESIDENTIAL

JOURNEY

OF

BARACK OBAMA

View from the Grassroots

PRESIDENTIAL

JOURNEY

OF

BARACK OBAMA

View from the Grassroots

STEVESON TERRELL

CONTENTS

To God
Be the Glory,
For great things He has done!

To Nita, Steve, Dani
My support group always!

To my inspiration for this book
President Barack Obama,
First Lady Michelle Obama and
First Daughters Malia and Sasha,
"Yes We Can!"

PREFACE

Presidential Journey of Barack Obama: View from the Grassroots is a sequential collection of provocative and prophetic political commentary that provides an insightful analysis of the campaign strategies used by Barack Obama, Hillary Clinton, John Edwards, and John McCain in their quests to become the 44th President of the United States.

The reader of this book will experience the heat, passion, and rapid heartbeat of the fiercely contested no holds barred 2008 presidential contest between Barack Obama, Hillary Clinton and John McCain. It was an exhilarating ride! I had a front row seat where my sight was never impeded by the trees and the forest was in full view at all times.

When the journey began, I was a committed Hillary Clinton supporter. I thought Hillary was the candidate who gave Democrats the best chance of winning back the White House. My early support of Hillary will be apparent to readers of the introductory chapters of this book. This is especially true of the early entry entitled *Hillary Can Boost Her Positives.*

However, things changed. When I perceived that the Clinton Campaign was mounting a sustained effort to create racial disharmony to gain a political advantage over Obama, my allegiance to Clinton came to an abrupt end. I divorced Hillary faster than Elizabeth Taylor divorced husbands. It was a decision I could endure because while I supported Hillary, I found Barack to be very appealing. As a matter of fact, during my advocacy for Hillary on my weblog, Leadership Cultivation.com, I repeatedly cautioned Hillary not to go negative towards Obama because I perceived that it would backfire. It was advice that was not followed and the result was disastrous for Hillary.

Like millions of other Americans who considered Obama, I came to the realization that Obama was uniquely qualified to lead America back to its position of honor and respect in the world. I was especially captivated by Obama's desire to have a United States of America instead of a dysfunctional set of red and blue states. Obama's vision for America moved me to action and I subsequently volunteered in his campaign.

I became a phone bank captain and member of the Obama army of small donors. Under my pen name, Bussta Brown, I used my Web presence on my blog, Leadership Cultivation.com and on Talking Points Memo.com (TPM), to be an unofficial Obama surrogate. Some of my blog posts were linked to political commentary on CNN and USA Today websites.

In addition to my website, my blogging experience on TPM was therapeutic because of the regular exchange it facilitated with other political junkies. Yet my most memorable campaign moment came when I participated in a conference call with future President Barack Obama on the weekend prior to Election Day. Mr. Obama told volunteers that he hadn't slept and advised us to keeping working hard in the final effort to win battleground states like North Carolina. His pep talk produced positive results.

Special Note: Underlined words in this book are active hyperlinks to more content which can be accessed on my weblog **LeadershipCultivation.com.** *Steveson Terrell*

CHAPTER 1 ~ October 2007

Obama, Hillary & Mrs. Edwards

In an obvious attempt by the John Edwards campaign to improve Edwards' chances of winning the 2008 Democratic Presidential Nomination, the Senator's wife, Mrs. Elizabeth Edwards, is serving as the attack dog, a role normally reserved for presidential running mates. First, it was the question of Obama's blackness and the country not honestly being ready for a Black president. Then it was the question of Hillary's unlikable factor which would surely motivate the Republican base to vote against her in record numbers. The conventional wisdom implied is that John Edwards is the most viable choice for the nomination with his status as the mainstream white male candidate. While I know that it's a political strategy being played out by the Edwards campaign, I can't help but reflect back on a scene from one of my all time favorite movies, "Blazing Saddles", the western film classic from Mel Brooks.

It's the scene where the good citizens of the all-white western town of Rock Ridge are anxiously awaiting the arrival of the new sheriff who unknowingly to them is Cleavon Little, who just happens to be Black. So when an orally-challenged cowboy in the lookout tower sees the Black sheriff approaching the town, he tries to warn the town folks that "The sheriff is ....." However, the town folks can't understand what the lookout is saying because the guy speaks gibberish and gets grounded out by noise generated by the excited crowd. The same thing needs to happen the next time that Mrs. Edwards declares that Obama is a Black man and Hillary is an unlikable woman.

Sidebar: Where is good old crowd background noise when you most need it?

President Al Gore?

This week, former U.S. Vice President Al Gore shared the Nobel Peace Prize for his efforts to combat global warming. With this latest award, the burning question again is will Al Gore jump in the race for President of the United States? Hillary Clinton has a commanding lead for the Democratic nomination and the awesome weapon of the still very popular former U.S. President Bill Clinton. Plus she has at her disposal, a potent political machine. To her credit, Hillary has looked presidential and has made no major missteps in her quest for the White House. While Barack Obama and John Edwards still offer challenges, Hillary will win hands down...unless of course Al Gore jumps in the race. At this point, Gore is the only candidate that still has a chance of derailing Hillary.

Governor Bill Richardson recently said that Hillary is acting like she has already won. Well, I think the handwriting really is on the wall. The race is about to be over in the first quarter. Obama and Edwards are showing signs of desperation and therefore are swinging harder for the fences. Both candidates are in attack mode and in the case of Edwards, he and his wife are conducting a tag-team assault. Adding to these two candidates' frustration is their awareness that if Hillary wins the nomination, neither of them is a viable running mate. With Obama, the naysayers will say that it is way too risky to have a Black male and a woman leading the Democratic ticket. And with Edwards, there is the perception that he brings no extra value, given that he did not help John Kerry make inroads in the South during the last election.

So again, for those who cannot or refuse to envision Hillary as the nominee, the spotlight is shining squarely on Al Gore. And in the case of Al Gore, one cannot help but wonder how does a person ever reconcile in their mind that they actually won the U.S. Presidency and did not get to serve in the office?

Sidebar: It's incomprehensible!

Mitt Romney's Criticism of Hillary's Values Is Weak

In addition to Hillary's Democratic opponents, it appears that the Republicans are also getting ready for the inevitable, a Hillary Clinton Presidency. The latest attack volley is Mitt Romney's criticism of Hillary's family values. Romney reasons that Hillary would set a bad example for our children if she gets in the White House. If I was Mitt, I would be more careful about casting unfounded criticism. He cites the last Clinton White House as a prime example of less than ethical values.

I vividly recall that before the current Republican president took office, similar comments were made about the need to restore honor to the White House. We all know how those promises turned out. Given the current state of affairs, I don't think we ever made it to the restoration point. Now are we really expected to give the Republicans another insincere try? Hillary at least deserves the chance to try to return this country to a more stable global status.

The different Republican strategies sometimes have bordered on being comedic. The Republicans' number one objective always was to keep Hillary from the top of the Democratic ticket. At first the Republicans tried to convince everyone that they wanted to run against Hillary. Not true. They still get nightmares when they recall what took place the last couple of times that they tangled with a Clinton. Now the Republicans are ramping up the strategy that Republicans run with extreme perfection, lies and innuendos. However, after eight years of disastrous Republican rule, Mitt's time would be better spent practicing saying "Madam President."

Sidebar: Even dogs will eventually stop salivating each time you ring the bell, if their expectations of a just reward repeatedly fails to materialize.

Hillary Clinton Can Boost Her Positives

This morning I had the distinct displeasure of listening to an interview of Jim Geraghty of the National Review on XM radio's P.O.T.U.S. 08. In essence, Mr. Geraghty appeared to encourage Hillary Clinton's closest Democratic opponents, Barack Obama and John Edwards, to increase negative attacks on her. Maybe Geraghty wasn't aware that historically launching an unwarranted negative attack against your opponent has been a Republican strategy, and these are Democrats.

Geraghty went on to argue that Hillary can't break 50 percent against any of her potential opponents including Ron Paul and that Democrats needed to see the light quickly. This guy was really spinning this morning. Well Jim let me give you some positives to consider. Hillary is the choice of most Democrats because of her strong points, skilled in governance, intelligence and leadership abilities. A lot of Hillary's so-called negative points are the product of an orchestrated relentless Republican smear and fabrications campaign (ala Swift Boat Veterans) conducted against her and her husband President Bill Clinton.

Hillary is leading because the country has become more comfortable with the prospect of a woman president. Jim, women are competence enough to lead. They lead in business, education, families, and in all walks of life. We are behind the British and the Germans in our acceptance of women serving as the leader of the national government. We live in an evolving society and the time has come to elect the United State's first woman president. My prediction is that Hillary Rodham Clinton will withstand Swift Boat Veteran type attacks, Rush

Limbaugh, Sean Hannity, Bill O'Reilly and Fox News to become that person in 2008.

Sidebar: The reason not to elect a woman president of the United States surely can't be that they will mess things up beyond comprehension. It's too late for that.

CHAPTER 2 ~ November 2007

Hillary, George 41, Newt, YouTube and GOP Spinners

Two weeks ago, I wrote about how Barack Obama and John Edwards had fallen further behind and would amp up the negative attacks on Hillary Clinton, mainly because neither candidate is a viable choice for running mate. For them it's either win or go home and the stay at home is probably going to be longer for Edwards than Obama.

What wasn't as clear at the time was the fear of Hillary that had also consumed the Republicans. At first the GOP had tried to be coy and had falsely portrayed that they wanted Hillary as the Democratic nominee. Psych! Hillary is their worst nightmare. So what did the Republicans do? After the latest debate, they enlisted George H.W. Bush and Newt Gingrich to sow seeds of doubt about her ability to sustain her enormous lead. They also used minions to attack the sincerity of her YouTube posts and instructed the ever-perched GOP Spin Doctors on Fox News to say to us, don't believe your lying ears and eyes.

Well the strategies are certainly getting more interesting by the day. However to her credit and as feared, Hillary is proving to be no pushover. She is gut punching her opponents. The lady does have a law degree from Yale and she is one to be reckoned with. So it's not going to be easy fellows. Hillary is not retiring quietly to the kitchen, or allowing herself to be relegated to watching the kids, cleaning the house or performing other stereotypical tasks that some men and women in this country think are reserve for women. Hillary is kicking butt and is headed straight for the residence at 1600 Pennsylvania Avenue.

Sidebar: The game is under two minutes. The opposition is showing its desperation by blitzing on every down. Can Hillary escape the blitz? She is going long, running the deep post pattern like Randy Moss! The Cover Two defense can't get there in time! She's in the weak spot...at the goal line! It's too late! She's in! Touchdown!

Election 2008 and the Overrated Independent or Swing Voter

During the last election we got beat over the head about the importance of the independent or swing voter. Flash back to the post debate studio audience interviews that had some participants still on the fence, undecided but leaning either Democratic or Republican even up until the eve of the election. They are the perpetual coin-flippers. Well excuse me if I don't wait on your decision before making up my mind. Talk about indecisiveness.

Now once again we get to hear about how this or that candidate has the majority of their party's votes but may not fare as well with independents or swing voters. Okay. There aren't a lot of secrets out there waiting to be uncovered. The U.S. has suffered on the world stage because of a lack of diplomacy, the economy could use a boost, poor kids don't have health insurance and trillions of dollars have been spent on a flawed military strategy that has neglected wounded and returning veterans.

Some political strategists including some reporters are attempting to distract us with polling numbers or meaningless intangibles such as likability factors possibly to prevent us from considering worthwhile traits such as leadership skills, competence or intelligence. We must insist on receiving objective reporting from mainstream media outlets. And lastly for the sanity of all, this time around let's resolve to not humor the attention-seeking independents or procrastinating undecided voters (who are probably faking anyhow), and adopt the theme, "Lead, Follow, or Get the Heck out of the Way."

Sidebar: In case you missed the point the first time, "Lead, Follow, or Get the Heck out of the Way."

Where in the World Is Senator Fred Thompson?

Some of us have wondered, "Where in the world is Waldo?" Currently, the same question can be asked about Fred Thompson, the former U.S. Senator from the state of Tennessee who incidentally has formally announced that he is a candidate from President of the United States. Waldo is yet to announce. Well political prognosticators had cautioned that with the advance billing that Fred Thompson was receiving prior to his announcement, it would be next to impossible for him to fill his own big shoes.

Fred Thompson was being portrayed as the candidate that the conservative wing of the Republican Party coveted the most. However, Thompson has been missing in action. It's been reported that there is little sign of life at his South Carolina HQ and it's been in operation for weeks. It's possible that Thompson's low profile has led to a crack in the dam. This week, Pat Robertson who is co-founder of the Christian Coalition endorsed the candidacy of Rudy Giuliani and it's rumored that James Dobson, the Focus on the Family founder, favors Mike Huckabee. Where does that leave Fred Thompson who had staked out the conservative faction of the GOP? It appears that where Thompson is concerned, the believers are behaving like non-believers.

In an interesting addition to the storyline, James Carville, the brilliant political strategist masquerading as a country bumpkin, has raised the possibility of the eventual GOP nominee being Jeb Bush. Shades of Al Gore! It's a brilliant strategy because just when the

Republicans are trying to gain traction through the emergence of a lead candidate, the Jeb Bush Factor delays solidarity and injects another option that the GOP must consider especially in light of their less than favorable current choices.

Sidebar: Now Hillary Clinton will not be the lone front-running candidate hearing footsteps in the distance.

Who Gains from a Weakened Obama Candidacy?

Barack Obama is under political siege because of his select status as someone who could win the Presidency of the United States. His patriotism is being questioned because he reportedly "didn't place his hand over his heart during the singing of the National Anthem" or because "he doesn't wear a U.S. Flag lapel pin." He has a Muslim name. He is a Black man. All is fair in love and war. Right? Well, let's explore who gains by a weakened Obama candidacy?

Hillary Clinton gains since Obama is close on her heels jockeying for the top spot. John Edwards gains because in most cases he is running third behind Clinton and Obama and wants to go head to head with Hillary without interference. Republicans gain when top Democrats become distrustful and suspicious of each other in a manner that ultimately prevents Party unity.

Talk radio and TV, spin doctors, surrogates, independent supporters will "innocently" raise suspicions or distort the truth in ways that insult the intelligence of the American people in attempts to gain advantage for the candidates of their choice. Just read the comments on the editorial pages or the biased political columns. If through their silence, presidential candidates passively sanction or tolerate deceptive campaign practices, there may be many possible gainers, but no winners. Most

Americans want to see integrity restored in the strategies used in the contest for the White House.

Regardless of the source, anyone running for President of the United States of America should immediately disavow and distance themselves from the despicable and dishonest tactics unleashed in recent days against Barack Obama.

Sidebar: Americans deserve and demand better politics!

After Nevada, Hillary Clinton is Still a Runaway Train

We know her simply as Hillary, the Clinton isn't necessary. She has celebrity status. Sound familiar? For months the Republican's main strategy was to pretend that they wanted Hillary so bad they could taste it. The truth is now and then, the Republicans want no parts of Hillary. They probably still experience night sweats from the Bill Clinton landslide that occurred in spite of their Ken Starr led campaign. I guess the only thing left to do after those results was to buy the media...but that's a story for another time.

The other truth for the Republicans is that even after months of spinning a bad story and trying to persuade Hillary's Democratic opponents to go negative against her (see "Hillary Can Boost Her Positives"), the gap between Hillary and her competition is widening. Witness the ineffectiveness of the negative strategy during the Nevada debate. Barack Obama and John Edwards got no traction and Edwards actually got booed. That's fitting punishment, because voting Democrats will reject the cornerstone strategy of every Republican campaign in recent memory.

The Democratic core insists that Democrats act like Democrats. During the last campaign, give Howard Dean credit for helping Democratic candidates find their backbones. So this is the dilemma. Obama and Edwards can't gain ground on Hillary by acting like Republicans and Hillary will lose her momentum if she pushes a largely Republican agenda. If indeed that becomes Hillary's prevailing strategy, she will still win the nomination, but almost certainly slow-leak the energy from the Democratic base will need to propel her to the U.S. Presidency in 2008. And read my prior post to find out how much value I think should be placed on courting so-called independent and undecided voters.

Sidebar: Buttering your bread on both sides can lead to messy results.

2008 Presidential Candidates Exposing Fear of Hillary, Increase Negativity

As if they were in the home stretch of the Kentucky Derby or the Indy 500, the 2008 Presidential Candidates are experiencing an adrenalin rush. The target in their sights is Hillary Clinton, the consensus frontrunner. Democrats and Republicans alike are running 24/7 campaigns of desperation to try and stop Hillary before it is too late. Their campaigns have increasingly gone negative (a traditional position for Republicans) and are filled with distortions and innuendos in attempts to create doubts about Hillary's electability. And being the boy scouts that they are, any one of them is more than willing to take her place in the front running position.

Hillary is correct to assert that the chief strategies being used by her fellow Democrats are etched in stone in the GOP playbook, because they are. Going negative has had some measure of success. Just ask John McCain about the results of the negative campaign run by George W. Bush against him in South Carolina or Michael Dukakis about what effect the Willie Horton ads had that were run against him by George H.W. Bush.

Here is the negative formula. Write or say something negative about your opponent or seize a trivial comment made by your opponent, take it out of context or simply overstate its importance in the greater scheme of things. Create rumors. Question your opponent's abilities while overlooking your own obvious shortcomings. Whatever the accusation, repeat it over and over and over again with the hope that it will be accepted as the truth. All too often, with the help of the media, this becomes the reality. Flashback to James Baker in the aftermath of the 2000 Election repeatedly saying, "We counted them...we counted them again and again and again."

Lastly, in a final show of desperation, circulate a picture of your opponent with persons of color or insinuate that he or she is too sympathetic to their interests. This strategy seems to work particularly well in the so-called Red States as insurance to get the vote out.

Well, it's very obvious that the chess match is in full effect. It will be interesting to see how Hillary responds. If Hillary goes negative too, she falls in the trap and places herself in check. Nonetheless, Hillary is still in the catbird seat, because as the Queen she is the most powerful player on the board with the ability to move in any direction. This characteristic alone is enough to strike fear in the hearts of Hillary's opponents. If Hillary makes the right moves, it's Check and Mate. Game over!

Sidebar: At this stage of the game, Hillary's opponents are hoping at least for a Stalemate.

Karl Rove's Advice for Hillary's Opponents Dissected...Dismissed

In the November 17, 2007 issue of <u>Newsweek</u>, Karl Rove wrote an opinionated column entitled, <u>How to Beat Hillary (Next) November.</u> Upon close review, I found the article contained the same old Republican strategy of negative attacks, distortions, and Swift Boating of your opponent. Below are some of the key points Mr. Rove advocated in his article along with my take on some things that remained unsaid. All text referenced is directly from Mr. Rove's November 17, 2007 <u>Newsweek</u> article.

First, Rove wants the GOP nominee to "Introduce [himself] again right after winning the nomination." I don't really know how this will help the Republican nominee because for the most part the American people will already know a lot about the nominee. Does Mr. Rove want the GOP nominee to misrepresent who he really is in order to increase his electability?

Second, "Say in authentic terms what you believe... [in order] to set up a natural contrast with [Hillary] Clinton." Here, Mr. Rove assumes that the American people (at least the Democrats) after having nominated Hillary will blot out all her favorable traits that will make her the best choice for President. Of course, here you can expect the GOP in a negative and distorted manner to try and redefine Hillary Clinton to the American people while trying to present their candidate in a more favorable light. Swift Boaters, please report front and center!

Third, "Tackle issue families care about." Now there's a novel ideal. I guess what Mr. Rove is saying is that after months of campaigning and years of building a track record that show that Republicans don't care about real family values, especially those of the American working class, say that you do. And we Americans being naive will embrace this new you and expect your true stripes to change once you get in office.

Fourth, "Campaign for the votes of minorities...." "Emphasize how your message can provide hope." Hope? This one really takes the cake. Republicans have shown that they do not care about minorities, just their votes. In one instance, the Republicans will play the race card i.e. Willie Horton, and then insist to minorities that they will represent their best interests (Of course, after the election). This is a huge insult.

Expect Republicans to use wedge issues like gay marriage and abortion to try and peel off a few minority voters. Republicans are good at trying to protect the unborn, but show little compassion for the well-being of babies that actually are born. Also pay very close attention to the Republican National Convention. It will be one of the most lacking in diversity events that you will see in 2008. Yet, the Republicans will still say to minority voters, don't believe your lying eyes.

Lastly, Rove writes, "Be strong on Iraq." This will be a hard sell for the Republicans to make because none of their potential candidates will be able to convince the American people that they are any stronger on national security than Hillary would be. Of all the reasons that the Republicans really would rather have Barack Obama or John Edwards to contend with as the Democratic nominee, this is the one. Republicans have spent a lot of energy attempting to vilify Hillary for being a non-traditional woman. This is where the strategy backfires. Their efforts have helped to cast Hillary as a very strong person, regardless of gender. She is strong enough in fact to serve as President of the United States.

Sorry Mr. Rove. If this is the best that the Republicans can muster, it's still going to be a lost cause for the GOP in 2008. Incidentally, the other well kept fear that Republicans have is that they don't relish facing another Clinton. Of all the words that can be used to describe the Clintons, (and you can bet that Rhodes Scholar Bill will be a key Hillary strategist) dumb and pushover, aren't included.

Sidebar: Fear the Clinton counterpunch. Stick and move.

Hillary Is Still Ahead

In recent days, the race for the 2008 Democratic Presidential Nomination appeared to have tightened. In response, it seems that Hillary Clinton is taking the bait to go negative. This she must not do in order to continue to separate herself from the pack. Going negative is a sure sign of a desperate campaign. Witness Barack Obama and to a greater extent John Edwards pulling out the Republican playbook. Obama is getting help from the Republicans who continue their strategy to help pick their opponent.

Hillary must continue to respond to all attacks to prevent any distortions from sticking, but in the case of Obama, sugar instead of salt will be much more effective. Obama is a very likable fellow and he is the future, but Hillary must keep smiling and communicate to people the reason why she is the now. In the end it will pay more dividends.

Sidebar: Hillary must remember that the world already knows that she is tough, but "sugar and spice and everything nice" is still the winning formula.

CHAPTER 3 ~ December 2007

Republicans Say What the Heck...Their Fear of Clinton Takes Center Stage

I have written for weeks about the Republican's not so secret strategy to handicap the 2008 presidential campaign by benignly promoting the selection of a Democratic presidential nominee that they perceive to be weaker than Hillary Clinton. Now Karl Rove and other Republicans are no longer trying to conceal their true motives. As revealed by recent actions, their not so secret objective is to promote the candidacy of Barack Obama who they feel would be a sitting duck. Now why do you suppose that to be the case? Well there is more to be said about that later. Rove has even gone public with instructional commentary and pep talks to Obama. What can we expect next, a contribution to the Obama campaign?

That is what I call the manifestation of fear. The GOP surrogates are relentlessly working the comment areas on the web, in newspapers and magazines, and perpetually are trying to gain traction with their overblown and overstated "America hates Hillary rhetoric." I read one comment that complained about Hillary trying to take us back to the 90's. And that was supposed to be a negative. Sorry pal, but compared with the last seven years, the Clinton 90's look pretty good to most Americans. Another strategy is to try to discredit CNN and Wolf Blitzer in particular by referring to CNN as the Clinton News Network. That one is so prevalent that it has to be on the Republican talking points FAQ. I guess CNN remains too much of an independent voice. To be in the Republican cross hairs, CNN must actually be still reporting the news.

So expect more tips from Rove with Obama as the beneficiary of choice. Why Obama? In present day

America, he is perfect for the GOP attack machine. There is his non-traditional name, the experience light, and did I mention that he is Black. As much as the progressive and admiring Anglo-Saxon public appears to be intrigued by Obama, in this country when it comes to Black candidates, rarely have the actual votes cast matched the projections or exit polls. And make no mistake about it. The Republican Party will play the race card. The only unknown variable is when. A good prediction would be close to election day, because the race card is not about swaying opinions, it is about igniting fears and prejudices that have been proven to be good catalysts for mobilizing the GOP base to the polls.

Sidebar: Can you say Jesse Jackson, Al Sharpton...Willie Horton? Incidentally, before Bush/Dukakis, the most famous Willie Horton played baseball for the Detroit Tigers.

Religious Conviction and the 2008 Elections

Religion and politics are strange bedfellows. Mitt Romney is a Mormon. Mike Huckabee is Southern Baptist. Hillary Clinton and Barack Obama are Protestants. Everybody is something, but it seems that the most important thing that the candidates want voters to know is that their religious beliefs will not factor into their decision making.

Okay let's rewind. If we pick and choose when our religious beliefs come into play in order to avoid conflict or offending someone who serves an opposing god, isn't that being a bit hypocritical. I know that the God of Christians is a jealous God. And while we may not hold animosity towards another's person-hood, we cannot serve or worship another God.

Now that is not to say that a non-Christian can't make social policy that benefits mankind. If the truth be known, sometimes confessing Christians make policy decisions that don't benefit mankind. Take for instance the case of abortion. Abortion is a terrible action. To me life begins at the point of conception the instant that the male sperm fertilizes the female egg. While many Christians adamantly oppose abortion, some of these same Christians are candidates or support candidates that turn a blind eye to the babies that actually are blessed enough to make it into the world. Go figure.

Some Christians fall ridiculously short when it comes to social policy. As a matter of fact, they can be the worst enemies of Christian values. I never understood the Moral Majority that supported and promoted immoral social policy. Doesn't every child deserve to have health care and shouldn't we be concerned with the plight of starving children? And we don't have to leave our shores to find starving children. They are right here in the United States, living in the neighborhood.

In the end, Christians are left to decide the weight that should be given to the religious beliefs held by their candidate of choice. I think it's a very important decision.

Sidebar: Does the concept, separation of church and state really exist, given that "... as [a man] thinketh in his heart, so is he." Proverbs 23:7 KJV

Hillary Needs to Keep Bill Clinton in the Game

Bill Clinton did exactly what the opposition doesn't want him to do when he appeared on the Charlie Rose Show big as life in support of his wife Hillary. Bill remains Hillary's best advocate and instead of being a shrinking violet, he should enlarge his involvement and presence in her campaign. And why shouldn't he tout her attributes? He is the person that has the most knowledge of her abilities.

Bill Clinton remains extremely popular within the Democratic Party. The prior two Democratic Presidential nominees made the mistake of distancing themselves from the former President with disastrous results. Hillary appears to be smart enough not to make the same mistake. At present, after a relentless assault from Democratic and Republican opponents alike, Hillary finds herself in a much tighter contest for the Democratic nomination. To her detriment, she took the bait and countered her attackers with somewhat negative assaults of her own. That was definitely the wrong strategy.

The right strategy is to use Bill Clinton more. None of her opponents has an adequate defense. Not even Oprah can neutralize that kind of firepower. In the final analysis, what can the opposition say if Hillary leans on her husband for support? Like the majority of married couples in the United States, husbands and wives do talk about important issues and often seek each other's advice. Another important point to make is that when Hillary was first lady, her critics wanted her to follow the typical first lady script of being the official host of White House tea parties. Hillary didn't conform to that model. Now her opponents want to portray her as a docile former presidential wife and she was anything but that. She acquired meaningful executive experience during the eight years that she occupied the White House with Bill Clinton.

Hillary should fire any campaign advisers that press her to minimize the presence of Bill Clinton. She should avoid making the mistake of not using her best offensive weapon before the opposition shows that they can stop it. Coaches often make this mistake or fail to use a weapon of which their opponents have knowledge. Hillary must keep her best team on the floor and say to the opposition "go ahead, take your best shot."

Sidebar: Only a fool would believe that when the outcome was on the line that Michael Jordan wasn't going to take the big shot or that Randy Moss wasn't going to get the deep pass. An even bigger fool was the one that failed to have their best weapon in the game.

2008 Presidential Candidates and Christmas

I don't like the Moral Majority, the Religious Right or the politics of the so-called Social Conservatives. I think these organizations and their advocates are often hypocritical and self-serving much in the same manner as the Pharisees and Publicans when they prayed in public places and extolled their virtues as not being "as other men." But the attribute that I do like is their boldness to say "Merry Christmas."

We have become too politically correct when we can't say Merry Christmas for fear of offending someone. The last time I checked, December 25 is listed as Christmas Day, not Happy Holidays Day. Democrats who like to play the field and sometimes be everything to everybody are especially timid when it comes to standing up for Christian traditions. We are so quick to defend every religion on Planet Earth; however it's not cool to be a Christian.

If you say Merry Christmas, you can expect to come under attack by your political rivals. Just ask Mike Huckabee. Mike might be playing politics too, but I do like his willing to say, "Merry Christmas." For President, I favor either of the Democratic big three, Hillary Clinton, Barack Obama and John Edwards, in that order. On the Republican side, it's only Mike Huckabee. A large reason for that is his religious background. My hope would be that Huckabee would have the conviction to practice Christian values that would serve to benefit mankind.

Will Democratic candidates allow Christianity to be staked out as being mutually exclusive to the GOP? Will Democrats defend Christian principles and reject the notion that Christianity can be watered down or cherry-picked to justify pet situations? The Bible recognizes sin as being sin without degrees. We are further called upon to repent of our sins in lieu of succumbing to our sins. So will Democratic candidates be bold enough to stand up when placed in a situation where the world expects them to waffle on Christian principles? It remains to be seen.

Sidebar: During this season as we celebrate the birth of a Savior who is Jesus the Christ, it's Merry Christmas!

Hillary Is Still the Best Choice

Much as I predicted in an earlier <u>post</u>, the race for the 2008 Democratic Nominee has tightened. With Hillary Clinton having a commanding lead the only recourse left for Barack Obama, John Edwards, and yes, the Republican Party was to mount an all out assault. The assault strategy would come straight from the GOP playbook. In a nutshell the strategy was to go negative, go negative, and go negative. For reasons unknown to me, that strategy seems to work well in this country.

Edwards went negative. Obama with coaxing from Karl Rove and the Republican Party went negative. The Republicans amped up their negative attacks. When Hillary countered her attackers with a negative strategy of her own, it backfired on her primarily because it tended to validate the fabrications which were being used against her. So now we have a tighter contest. Let's explore how Hillary got into this predicament of losing ground to her opponents.

Hillary should not have voted for the War in Iraq, but she had plenty of company. She is also currently being portrayed as a typical First Lady and she was anything but. As a matter of fact, she was raked over the coals because she tried to push through a program that would make health insurance available to every American. How selfish can you be? Isn't the theme of this country, survival of the fittest? How could any politician be naive enough or have the compassion to think that people who could not afford health insurance shouldn't be left to fend for themselves? How could Hillary have the audacity to think that we, the American people, could rise above our own selfish little motives and be our brother's keepers?

Well it remains to be seen how things will turn out, but Hillary is still the best choice. The Republicans have had America on the wrong course for the last seven years. It's up to the Democrats to get this country back on the right track and Democrats need their strongest and most qualified candidate running in the general election. Hillary may not have the experience of a Joe Biden, Chris Dodd or Bill Richardson, but of the top-tier candidates, she is the most qualified and has the best chance of being elected president in November 2008.

Sidebar: Again my advice to Hillary is to stay the course and if the need arises for a response to negative attacks, do so in a straightforward and positive manner. And everyone knows that you must respond to attacks or you will surely become the prey of the Swift-Boaters.

CHAPTER 4 ~ January 2008

Republicans Want Obama

Barack Obama now leads in Iowa over Hillary Clinton and John Edwards largely due to the support he is getting from "Independent" voters. After a <u>concerted effort</u> to push Obama to the front of the pack, the Republicans must be overjoyed. It's not joy because Republicans like Obama better than the other Democratic frontrunners, but rather joy because the Republicans think that Obama would be the easier mark in the 2008 General Election.

Independent voters in Iowa may actually be Republican wolves in sheep's clothing trying to handicap the contest. No question, that's been the ongoing strategy of that very tricky GOP. But as Robert Burns wrote in his poem "<u>To A Mouse</u>", "The best laid [plans] of mice and men [often go astray]." In other words, Republicans better be careful for what they wish. No matter which Democratic candidate eventually ends up as the nominee, the GOP after displaying such incompetence running the country, will have a tough row to hoe in their quest to return another Republican to the Oval Office anytime in the near future because America has awaken.

Sidebar: "You Can't Have Your Cake and Eat It Too."

Huckabee Wins Iowa

<u>Mike Huckabee</u> won the Iowa Caucuses. That's a significant achievement for someone who was once in the second or even third tier of the Republican candidates. Mitt Romney must be highly disappointed since he fully embraced the Republican strategy of attempting to tar and feather your opponent. His strategy of closely aligning himself with President Bush was also a huge failure.

I think that Huckabee won because he didn't shy away from his faith and the country does want leaders who practice some degree of civility. The challenge for Huckabee will come later. He will now have the bull's eye squarely on his chest. I don't think that Republican candidates can stop themselves from going negative. Although Republican candidates usually aren't hesitant in gut punching an opponent in order to win, I think it was a good decision by Mike Huckabee to pull a negative ad which he had planned to run.

Huckabee has wide appeal largely because he comes across somewhat as a nice guy. But now as other Republicans jump on his winning bandwagon, because everyone loves a winner, Huckabee must reject some traditional Republican strategies of fabricating and promoting wedge issues and race-baiting.

Sidebar: Resisting that race-baiting thing will be especially hard if the Republican's Democratic opponent ends up being <u>Barack Obama</u>.

Iowa Caucus Results Analyzed and the Theme Is Change

The Iowa results are in and the dynamics of the 2008 U.S. Presidential Campaign have changed dramatically. Tonight, the candidates made some of the best speeches that I have heard them make. John Edwards made a very good speech. He talked about change and appeared to try and dismiss Hillary Clinton to reshape the contest as a race between himself and Barack Obama. The jury is still out on that one. In another strategic move, I think John decided to leap forward early to claim second place while he was actually in second place fearing that his status could change. With money as an object though, it will be interesting to see where his campaign goes from here. Then on the other hand, the money handicap didn't sink Mike Huckabee.

Hillary Clinton made a very good and upbeat speech and I disagree with the commentators opinions that she or Bill Clinton showed devastation in their demeanors. I think she also staked out her position as a change agent along with the other candidates. I lot was read into the results that weren't there and I think that some of the commentators' obvious dislike of the Clintons morphed them into spin doctors. <u>Bill Clinton</u> is still a great weapon for Hillary and her campaign shouldn't take the bait and diminish his role. When presented with the opportunity, the Clinton campaign have failed to remind folks that when the pundits talk about this great need for change, it's more a rejection of the Bush years rather than the Clinton years when America enjoyed a consistent period of prosperity.

My advice also to Hillary is that she needs to quickly inject some youth in her campaign. I understand and respect the need to shelter your child, but Chelsea could help in this regard with a more visible role in Hillary's campaign. Another thing that Hillary needs to be more aware of is that some women (including some prominent commentators) appear to be acting out the "crabs in a barrel syndrome" when it comes to her candidacy.

Barack Obama made a great and inspiring speech ala Dr. King, and he will get a tremendous boost coming out of Iowa. Obama really owned the stage and seized the moment. It was obvious that he is more confident on the big stage instead of in a debate setting where he appeared at times to be unsure of himself. Tonight Obama made people believe that he can actual win the U.S. Presidency. And perception is reality. As a result, especially in South Carolina, Obama will be a much stronger option for Black voters who will enthusiastically support a winner.

On the Republican side, the likable preacher Mike Huckabee also gave an outstanding and inspiring speech. He was inclusive and appeared to speak from the heart. I think that Mike Huckabee showed that being bold with your <u>Christian</u> faith doesn't have to be a liability. I predict that he will grow in statue and develop a broader national appeal as Americans pay him closer attention. And much like the Obama campaign, as the attention turns to New Hampshire, the Iowa results will also boost his campaign and more folks will embrace the possibility of Huckabee being the Republican nominee. However for Huckabee, certain factions of his own party will aggressively seek to let the air out of his sail.

On the other hand, Mitt Romney may have talked about change, but with his close alignment and defense of the current Republican Administration, he represents more of the status quo. For Romney, it's do well in New Hampshire or go home. In addition to coming across as a corporate stuffed shirt, his biggest handicap may be that he is a Mormon. As much as people will embrace Romney openly and say that his religion doesn't matter, they will mobilize, go behind closed curtains and vote the other way.

Sidebar: As Hillary, Obama, and Huckabee battle to take up residence at 1600 Pennsylvania Avenue, they must find ways to neutralize the other crabs in their barrels.

Hillary Really Is the Comeback Kid!

Tonight the reported demise of Hillary Clinton as a continued viable candidate for the 2008 Democratic Presidential Nomination proved to be premature. There is a collective shock in America that Hillary Clinton won the New Hampshire Democratic Primary. After being counted out by her usual flock of detractors who had projected her to lose by double-digits to Barack Obama, Hillary emerged victorious. John Edwards, who after Iowa had asserted that the race had become a two-person contest between he and Obama, finished a distant third.

In a bit of a role reversal, Hillary who once was the inevitable Democratic nominee beat the latest inevitable nominee, Barack Obama. Now it really is a competition. It's a competition to the chagrin of the Republican Party that will help the ultimate Democratic winner be tougher to beat in November 2008. The GOP strategist and Karl Rove must be in shock and scratching their heads. I stand by my earlier claim that Republicans fear a contest against Hillary Clinton.

Resilience is the word. Hillary in short order has retooled. Once down, she is far from being out. In New Hampshire, the Clinton counter-punch was in full effect. Hillary fought for and won the support of women and especially the young people. In contrast to last week in Iowa, Hillary's on-stage backdrop for her victory speech had the symbolism of youthful vitality. Chelsea and Bill (yes Bill) were also close by her side. Most of the political commentators ended up with egg on their faces. And much to my personal satisfaction, the pollsters and Hillary's many haters got it wrong and shared the sunny-side up meal of the commentators. Hillary must be chuckling to herself. Good for her.

My latest advice to Hillary is not to listen to the pundits, but keep Bill highly involved in her campaign if not highly visible. Also, don't run away from being a woman. Stand tall and be proud. You are a woman who is very accomplished and very competence as well. And once again, my most pointed advice is avoid the Republican strategy of going negative or getting personal with her opponents, especially the very likable Barack Obama. This strategy **will** only backfire, alienate and weaken support with Black people and some women voters. Enthusiasm and not contempt from these support groups will be needed for Hillary to win in the general election.

Sidebar: Now it's on to South Carolina and Nevada for the rubber matches where the importance of the <u>overrated</u> independent voters will be further discredited. And did I forget to mention how personally gratifying it is that the pundits and Hillary haters were proved wrong.

What Is Karl Rove Up to Now?

After taking great pain to build Barack Obama up and provide <u>advice</u> to him about how to defeat Hillary Clinton, Karl Rove is now seeking to cast doubt upon Obama by assailing him with pointed criticism which amounts to him being inept in running a smart campaign. After Obama's lost to Clinton in New Hampshire, Rove in a <u>Wall Street Journal</u> article attempts to use reverse psychology to bait Obama into running an even more spirited negative campaign against his able opponent Clinton. To the unsuspecting, it's a brilliant strategy. But to the skeptical, it's hard to believe that Rove suddenly views Obama as "lazy" and reminiscent of "Adlai Stevenson."

Rove wants to ensure that Clinton and Obama are engaged in a ferocious dogfight throughout the campaign season that will leave both candidates with irreconcilable and irreversible damage going into November. Rove the ever sly instigator also claims that Hillary "lets her [dislike for Obama] show" by mentioning Obama last in her New Hampshire victory speech. What Rove fails to mention is that Hillary listed her opponents in what appeared to be reverse order of their perceived electability as evidenced by her reference to John Edwards just prior to Obama. It will be interesting to see if Clinton and Obama strategists are smart enough to see through the fog and avoid the latest Republican booby trap designed to provide sound bite material to fuel the GOP attack ads that await the eventual Democratic Presidential nominee.

Sidebar: Democrats will find it hard to convince discerning voters that <u>negative attacks</u> are unique to the Republican playbook, if the only real difference is that the Republican playbook is red and the Democratic playbook is blue.

Clinton and Obama: The Real Strategy

With the recent injection of race into the Democratic Presidential contest, we are left to scratch our heads in disbelief of the brain thrust of each candidate. What were they thinking? Frankly, I think it was strategy that backfired. Let's look at what could have occurred.

I think that the Clintons injected race to solidify their status with white voters in South Carolina knowing that they wouldn't completely alienate the support they enjoy from black people. The analogy between Dr. King and President Johnson wasn't necessary. The metaphoric use of "fairy tale" also wasn't necessary. Purposeful or happenstance, both actions unnecessarily divided voters along racial lines and that's a surefire recipe for a <u>GOP</u> victory in November.

With respect to Obama, the race incident tended to solidify his support with Black voters some of whom continue to question if Obama is "Black enough" as opposed to being too mainstream. This segment of voters should be smart enough to know that America is not going to embrace the Black person running for president to become the Black president. It's just not going to happen.

So after the latest attempts by Clinton and Obama to play nice, I hope that both campaigns get their messages back on the high road.

Sidebar: To remain or ascend to the status of <u>genius</u>, one should be required to perform as a genius. One more suggestion, keep the surrogates on the sidelines.

The GOP Dilemma: Hillary Clinton or Barack Obama

In the Keneen Ivory Wayans Satire Movie, "I'm Gonna Git You Sucka", two local hoods after being cornered were given the choice of leaving the building by "taking the stairs or the window", upon which they quickly chose the stairs. Fast forward to the next scene and the hoods are seen painfully tumbling down the stairs presumably after being forcibly pushed. For them, either of their available options, the window or the stairs, would lead to a bad outcome. Theirs were a no-win situation.

There is a similar dilemma facing the Republicans in the 2008 Presidential Sweepstakes. In the race for the White House, the GOP is pondering whether their weakest Democratic opponent would be Hillary Clinton or <u>Barack Obama</u>? After months of having high profile Republicans and their surrogates begging for <u>Hillary</u> with the hope of actually getting anyone but Hillary, evidence is growing that a head-to-head contest against Obama in the general election could prove to be just as difficult.

Judging by the strategic criticism and negative assaults being heaped upon Hillary and Obama recently by <u>Karl Rove</u>, it seems that the Republicans now equally <u>fear</u> both Democratic candidates. What is a person to do? Is it the window or the stairs? Is it Hillary Clinton or Barack Obama? Either choice is going to lead to an undesired outcome in November 2008 for the GOP.

Sidebar: O woe is me. But you reap what you sow.

Presidential Politics Makes Progress on Race

The <u>slugfest</u> between Hillary Clinton and Barack Obama has gained a lot of attention. It's an amazing thing. It's not amazing because the top two Democratic presidential candidates are taking each other to task on key campaign issues, but it's amazing because the top two Democratic candidates happen to be a woman and a Black man. Dr. Martin Luther King, Jr. would surely be proud. And unless John Edwards makes an equally amazing comeback, Clinton or Obama will become the Democratic nominee.

At work for these two contenders are racial and gender pride. To Obama's credit, he is viewed as a serious candidate and a recent CNN <u>poll</u>, suggests that White Americans are becoming more and more comfortable with the real possibility that a Black male could become President and a majority feels that the country is ready. Now that's progress. Happy Dr. Martin Luther King, Jr. Day.

The Case for Bill Clinton

In the months leading up to the start of the race for the White House, the Republican Party ran an aggressive undertaking to inflict major damage to the prospect of a Hillary Clinton for President Campaign. There was talk about her presence as a polarizing figure or her low likability factor that would ensure an energized Republican base of opposition. However, when you look <u>below the surface</u>, the GOP's real motivation was that they did not to run against Hillary Clinton and to be more specific, her chief advocate, <u>Bill Clinton</u>.

As we watch Hillary battle Barack Obama for the Democratic nomination, we clearly see why the GOP had reason to be intimidated. Bill Clinton is a master political strategist and his goal right now to get Hillary Clinton elected president of the United States. Early in the contest, Hillary had worn the aura of inevitability. For Obama and John Edwards, the contest was almost over before it got started. To stay competitive, Obama and Edwards unleashed their own negative attacks on Hillary, in effect joining the <u>assault</u> already coming from the Republican Party. Their <u>strategy</u> was successful and Obama in particular closed the gap on Hillary. But the real wake up call for the Clintons came when Obama won the Iowa Caucus. Suddenly, the Hillary Clinton candidacy was in trouble.

Political pundits quickly jumped on the Obama bandwagon and declared Hillary's campaign to be in trouble and predicted that real damage would occur if Hillary lost to Obama in New Hampshire. The Clinton Campaign got the message and unleashed their big gun, Bill Clinton who directed a Machiavellian strategic plan. This meant big trouble ahead for the competition. A <u>racial</u> element was injected into the campaign when the words of Hillary were deemed to disrespect the legacy of Dr. Martin Luther King, Jr. and Bill used risky political doublespeak when he appeared to minimize the viability of Obama while positioning Hillary as the white candidate running against the upstart black guy. In both instances, Obama seemed to fan the flames in order to benefit his candidacy and increase his stature in the Black community of South Carolina. Also, the Clinton campaign put on a full court press for women and younger voters. The strategy worked to perfection and victory was had in New Hampshire.

Smelling blood, the Clintons went for the kill. They have kept <u>constant pressure</u> on Obama. Now the Obama Campaign response is to complain along with an able assist from some political pundits, that the contest is unfair because of the increased presence of Bill Clinton. I think part of the Obama counter-strategy is to portray Bill Clinton's level of intervention as <u>unprecedented</u> by a former President. I think the criticism is unfounded because it fails to recognize that Hillary Clinton's candidacy is equally unprecedented. It is <u>unreasonable</u> and unrealistic to think that Bill Clinton doesn't have the right to come to the defense of his wife. As a matter of fact, his actions validate the reasons that companies feel that a nepotism policy is necessary. When a family member is attacked no matter the context, it's personal and the normal rules will not apply.

So Barack Obama is facing the Clinton monster up close and personal. And let's not forget that the Obama campaign fired the first volley. Their problem is they failed to account for the old neighborhood axiom, "you have to bring butt to kick butt." If you dish it out, you better be able to take it. In other words, what goes around comes around. Right now the Obama defense team doesn't appear to be up to the task. On the other hand, the Clinton strategy is until your hapless defense can stop us, we're going to run the same play over and over again.

So don't expect Bill Clinton to take himself out of the game until mission accomplished. Bill Clinton is Michael Jordan and the Chicago Bulls, Tiger Woods, Dean Smith's Carolina Tarheels and John Wooden's UCLA Bruins. They're going to regularly beat the crap out of you and there is absolutely nothing that you can do to prevent it.

Sidebar: All is fair in love and war and this is war.

Despite Obama Win in SC, Clinton Gameplan Unchanged

Before the Iowa Caucuses, Hillary Clinton enjoyed the status of being the inevitable 2008 Democratic Presidential Nominee. However, the campaign assaults conducted against her by Barack Obama, John Edwards and Republicans proved to be highly successful. This success did not escape the attention of the Clintons who responded in-kind by unleashing their own aggressive counter-offensive.

The Clintons' counter-offensive surprisingly included their own version of the "Southern Strategy" normally implored by Republicans. They cast Obama as the "black candidate", deducing that although Black voters would be turned off, offsetting gains would be made in the White and Hispanic communities. The strategy worked in New Hampshire and the Clintons wrote off South Carolina in the process as they turned their attention to Super Tuesday.

Against that backdrop, where are we now? Well, the Clintons are showing why the GOP feared running against them in the first place. They analyze situations quickly and make adjustments on the fly, usually faster than the opposition can react. It remains to be seen if their strategy will work? Stay tuned for the answer. One thing is certain. Their strategy is comprehensive and the Clintons will stay the course. Despite calls for the contrary, the chief strategist Bill Clinton will continue to bat clean-up.

Talking heads would have the masses believe that commentators and pundits can define the behavior and limits of former presidents. Nothing is further from the truth. Former Presidents, with their unique status, create their own paradigm. President Jimmy Carter, the tireless volume builder of Habitat for Humanity houses, quickly comes to mind in that regard.

So expect Team Clinton to use whatever strategy they deem necessary, even presumed race baiting, in order to propel Hillary Clinton to the White House. The Clinton campaign expects to retain a reasonable percent of Black voter support, but their short-term goal is to build a winning combination of traditional White and Hispanic voters. Furthermore, if the Clintons' strategy is successful and John McCain ends up as their GOP opponent, expect Geritol to become a household word.

Sidebar: The Clinton rally cry is <u>whatever it takes</u> and it's difficult to argue with a team batting one thousand in U.S. Presidential Elections.

Would Ted Kennedy Have Played the Race Card?

In the old western movies, sometimes the star or lead character was cast in the role of villain. In most cases before the end of the movie, the villain ultimately made the transition from bad to good guy. However despite their proverbial "<u>seeing the light</u>", the bad guys were never allowed to escape punishment for their transgressions, because of the mixed message that it would send.

Fast forward to today. After losing to Barack Obama in Iowa, and casting herself as a change agent, Hillary's campaign led by Bill Clinton, can be argued deliberately <u>injected race</u> into the contest for the Democratic nomination. Of course, the Clintons have categorically denied that this was the case. However, their denial was weakened by Bill Clinton's subsequent comparison of Obama to <u>Jesse Jackson</u> after Obama's victory in South Carolina.

This was mission accomplished. The voting <u>demographics</u> tended to support this line of thinking. It appears, the Clintons <u>succeeded in casting</u> Hillary as the traditional White candidate running against the anomaly Black candidate foolish enough to think that they can contend seriously for the White House. Hillary got the majority of the White vote and Obama increased his share of Black voters who may have been disenfranchised by Bill Clinton's recent comments.

This retro strategy that Bill Clinton spearheaded was especially troubling. Even though we know it was <u>just politics</u>, Black voters were used as pawns in a bigger endgame. To me, this raises a question of integrity and disloyalty. When Bill Clinton was beat down unmercifully by his enemies, Black people flocked to his rescue and never wavered in their support of him. This support was extended also to his wife, Hillary. So no matter the motive, Bill Clinton's rhetoric behavior was disappointing.

Now it begs the question. Since the Kennedy family is also held in high esteem by Black people in this country, would Ted Kennedy have played the race card? Kennedy, the elder statesman of the Democratic Party, reportedly had been very upset that Bill Clinton had injected race into the campaign. In a clear sign of his angst, Ted Kennedy on Monday <u>endorsed</u> Barack Obama. So I'm left to conclude that Ted Kennedy, if placed in a situation similar to the one that Hillary found herself after Iowa, would not have played the race card.

Sidebar: Like the star villains of old, it remains to be seen if Hillary and Bill will be held accountable and punished for their transgressions.

CHAPTER 5 ~ February 2008

Obama as President No Longer a Fairy Tale

My opinion about the electability of Barack Obama to serve as President of the United States has changed. After months of thinking to the contrary, I now think that Obama has a chance. At least I'm willing to commit a vote to finding out. Obama has been amazing. Obama has surprised a lot of people including many opponents whom I felt at one time saw him as an <u>easy mark.</u>

I hope that the country finally is at a place where race really doesn't matter. I hope it has become a place where white voters are truthful about their voting intentions. We know that all of the country isn't there. Barack doesn't do as well with older white voters as he does with the young who tend to be more accepting of racial differences.

Previously, I felt that a Clinton/Obama or an Obama/Clinton ticket would not be wise and did not have much of a chance of being successful. I have changed my mind in that regard also. The country is acting like it might be ready to grow up and rewrite history. A popular song reminds us that "<u>Everything Must Change.</u>" Although I remain somewhat of a skeptic, increasingly more and more Americans are becoming excited about the prospects of Obama being President and I too am willing to "<u>roll the dice</u>" on the young upstart who has so much potential.

I admit that my willingness to take a chance on Obama is influenced by the Clintons willingness to treat their Black support worst than a <u>jilted lover.</u> And like that jilted lover, once trust is betrayed, the relationship just doesn't feel the same anymore. You actually start to look at other suitors more objectively and the door opening to a different relationship has a greater possibility. Hillary had better hope that if she ends up as the Democratic nominee, that enough Black voters are willing to overlook the Clintons' recent transgressions and support her enthusiastically at the polls. That remains to be seen.

Sidebar: The political meal that Hillary Clinton has chosen contains White and Latino voters, with Black voters placed on the side.

Obama Could Get to the Promised Land

As a former heavily leaning supporter of Hillary Clinton for President, I have to admit that I'm a Johnny come lately to the Barack Obama bandwagon. However, it's better late than never. When Obama gave his victory speech after his big wins on Super Tuesday, I too was inspired. I too believe that Obama can become President of these United States and unite the country or in the least take us to a plateau that we have never been. More than any of the other candidates, Obama really does represent change. Obama can get to the Promised Land.

I still think that Hillary Clinton would also make a good President. She is smart, confident and quick on her feet. I think that she did acquire experience being in the White House with Bill for eight years. I for one think that the Clinton years were a period of prosperity for the U.S. and also a time of relative peace. And there is also the experience Hillary has gained in the U.S. Senate.

On the flip side, Hillary is tied too closely with the past. It's a past when Democrats and Republicans cannot collaborate for the common good. It's a time of gridlock. It's a time when poll numbers mean more than the poor. It's a time when winning trumps common sense. It's a time when the desire to win will allow you to turn your back on old friends.

Hillary and Bill did the unthinkable when they themselves went to the Republican playbook and pulled out the Southern Strategy of race baiting. With that decision, Hillary Clinton forfeited the right to be called an agent of change, but deserved to be held accountable. Before the race-baiting, Black voters were torn between Hillary and Barack. However, Obama's victories in the South where he received eight of ten Black votes that were cast showed that Black people are torn no longer.

Black voters have reacted to the Clinton's Southern Strategy like jilted lovers. Like a jilted lovers, although you still may love the person and truly want and need to get past the hurt, the offense festers and the angrier you get. That's the situation for Black voters right now, mad as hell. Mad enough in fact to embrace Obama and be optimistic enough to think that the future is now.

Barack Obama can be another John F. Kennedy or a Martin Luther King, Jr. Both men were young, both men dared to make a difference and both men left lasting legacies of having inspired a nation to do great things. I think that Obama is in that favored stratosphere. We can only hope that if Obama is the Democratic nominee that Republicans will not attempt to divide the electorate along racial lines. Oh I forgot that Clintons have already done the GOP that favor.

Sidebar: Think about it. If Hillary Clinton wins the presidency without strong support from the Black community, she will be free to govern from the center and start on Day One, running for re-election (yes re-election) without the obligation of serving as an advocate for what commentator Tavis Smiley calls the "Covenant with Black America."

Hillary and Barack May Need to Coexist

In the race for the White House on the Democratic side, I thought that at this point in the contest, Hillary Clinton would be taking victory laps. How wrong I was. I miscalculated. Barack Obama is in the stretch run with Hillary and if you haven't realized it already, Barack could win. Bill and Hillary know that he can win and that reality drove the Clintons to try and define the race in terms of black and white (and brown) after losing in Iowa. Because of a "lingering resentment" of that strategy being employed, this contest is not sewn up by Hillary and will proceed unsettled towards the Democratic Convention.

That situation possibly means that the Democratic Convention will be divided. The Democrats will need to get it together and the best way to achieve that goal may be a Clinton/Obama ticket or Obama/Clinton ticket. Although this ticket may allow the Democrats the best chance of winning in November, theirs is not the best team for governance in the White House. Neither one of these persons could stomach playing second fiddle to the other. That's a recipe for trouble and disharmony.

Sidebar: Check that. The team of three, Barack, Hillary and Bill would find it next to impossible to coexist in the White House.

Bill Clinton Is Not a Racist

On Fox News Sunday, during an interview with Chris Wallace, President Bush volunteered that Bill Clinton is not a racist. I don't know why the President made the statement except maybe to keep it part of the active campaign. I don't think that President Clinton is a racist either and the accusation is not a fair one. However, I do think that he used race-baiting as a campaign strategy. I think that most black people wanted to give Bill Clinton the benefit of the doubt after his "fairy tale" reference when speaking about Barack Obama and also after

Hillary's perceived insult to the legacy of Dr. Martin Luther King, Jr. And then there was the reference Bill Clinton made comparing Jesse Jackson and Obama after Obama's win in South Carolina. Now that was the straw that broke the camel's back. It angered a lot of people, not just Black voters who have responded with a vengeance.

So I want to make it clear that a lot of Black people don't think that Bill is a racist, but are highly disappointed in his recent behavior. The use of <u>race-baiting</u> puts Hillary somewhat with the Republican's camp and compromises her ability to get people to believe her claim that she represents change when her campaign uses old tactics. It's a strategy designed to divide and conquer. The Republicans use it to perfection to solidify and keep their Southern base intact. And a lot of the Republicans that use the "Southern Strategy" aren't racist either. But history has shown that some Republicans and now it appears Bill Clinton also, are willing to do almost anything to win an election.

Sidebar: It remains to be seen if Bill or Hillary Clinton can recover from their tactical blunder. One is also left to ponder whether the planned coalition of White women and Latino support is considered by the Clinton Campaign to still be on course.

Obama Is a Phenomenon

When Vince Carter arrived in the NBA fresh out of the University of North Carolina, he sat the league on fire. He was sensational. Each of his games was a new highlight film. ESPN featured his high-flying dunks and drives to the basket under a special category on their website. He brought new meaning to the word, postered. He dunked on Shaq, Mourning, Mutumbo, any and everybody who got in his way on the path to the basketball rim. He was a phenom.

Louisiana, Nebraska, Washington, Maine, and for good measure, the U.S. Virgin Islands are not the names of basketball players, but states that Barack Obama swept this past weekend for caucus or primary victories. It is called momentum and Obama has it. What he has been able to accomplish defies logic and is simply amazing.

After being built up by Republicans who thought they wanted to face him rather than Hillary Clinton in the general election and after being taken too lightly by his Democratic opponents, Obama has made believers out of all. He is a piped piper who is leading a transformation of the American society and mindset. He has a pretty good opponent in Hillary Clinton, but Obama is a phenomenon. While Hillary makes the All-Star Team, Obama gets the special and sometimes phantom calls reserved for the superstars.

So while the competition complains that he is all talk and little substance, most people are too enamored by his presence and the positive vibes that reverberates from him, that no one seems to be listening, and no one seems to care.

Sidebar: If Obama's momentum is not quickly derailed and Hillary ends up losing Ohio, Pennsylvania, or Texas, superdelegates will not be able to deliver on her presidential aspirations.

Barack Obama Leads a Movement

Tonight, I listened in awe as Barack Obama gave his victory speech in Madison, Wisconsin. In the audience, I saw Black and White, young and old, blue collar and white collar, and some people moved to tears as Obama spoke. They seemed to embrace the notion that America is ready for real change and that they can be a part of it. In other words, they can participate in a movement that will make this country better. They can be make history.

As Obama spoke, I saw a crowd that appeared to move mentally and spiritually inside the picture of possibilities that Obama so eloquently painted for them. It was truly amazing and gratifying to think that America could move to a higher plain. It's a higher plain where there is less political strife and more collaboration for the common good. It's a higher plain where people actually want to live together in peace and harmony. A higher plain where we as Americans care more about each other and come together to solve problems regardless of race, religion, political party affiliation, or economic status.

With Obama, we see that plateau as a possibility that we can experience and we want that experience also for our children. For too long, we have been running in place, but Obama represents real change. Obama has all the candidates talking about change because they see it as good politics given the connection Obama has made with the American people. But some of them seem to embrace the concept in name only. Witness Hillary Clinton, a person whom I admire and think could be a wonderful president. When Hillary's campaign appeared to falter, she turned to a <u>ridiculous and divisive strategy</u> that alienated Black voters in order to appeal to White and Latino voters. That's not change.

So as much as I personally admire Hillary and Bill Clinton, I think that the prospect of real hope and positive change is personified by Barack Obama. And as Obama said tonight, he realizes that change will not come easy. And if Obama indeed becomes the nominee, forces and principalities in high places will work day and night to try and prevent him from being successful in his goal to unify the country. However, Obama reminds us that we the people can force the issue and be a firewall against naysayers and against those who prey upon and profit from the misfortunes of others. Tonight, I saw Barack Obama leading a movement.

Sidebar: Tonight, I saw it in their faces and I can't see the people of Ohio, Pennsylvania or Texas being any less affected or hopeful of the change that Barack Obama represents. Tonight, I saw it in their faces.

Clinton's Last Stand

Reminiscent of General Custer at the Little Big Horn, Texas is where Hillary Clinton will make her last stand. Barack Obama has Hillary surrounded and is preparing to mount a contest ending assault. No one would have predicted that the Clinton campaign would be on the ropes at this juncture. It was supposed to be the other way around.

Momentum is a funny thing. It defies logic. People like a winner and Obama is undeniably a winner after eight straight wins. At the rate he is going, he may win Ohio, Texas and Pennsylvania, the latter despite Gov. Rendell's latest revelation.

Hillary's battle cry may be "Remember the Alamo", but if my memory serves me right, I don't think that the combatants actually survived the Alamo. The stark reality for Hillary and Bill Clinton is that the race to determine the 2008 Democratic Presidential Nominee may be over and Hillary will not win.

Sidebar: If previous tactics used by the Clinton campaign offer a clue, expect things to get real ugly for Obama in the days leading up to the next primaries.

Election 2008: When Is Change Not Change?

When is change not change? I guess it's when your opponent has such a lock on the concept that anything and everything must be done to discredit it. As Isaac

Hayes might say, "I'm talking about [change], shut your mouth." Barack Obama has voters wistfully thinking about the possibilities of historic change. When he made his victory speech after sweeping the "Potomac Primary", some persons had tears in their eyes, because with his words he painted such a vivid picture of a brighter future for America, and a brighter future for the world.

So how did Obama's opponents respond to his message of hope? Well Republican John McCain basically told an audience made up mostly of senior citizens of the GOP, not to have hope. I guess that's why Senator McCain said that we could be in Iraq for a <u>hundred years.</u> I guess he never read the Dr. Spencer Johnson book "Who Moved My Cheese", wherein one of the main characters perished when they didn't have the courage or vision to move beyond their current plight. When McCain looks into the tunnel, he probably sees no light at the end. From that viewpoint, why waste time on hope.

Obama's fellow Democrat, Hillary Clinton, is now calling Obama's version of change, "empty rhetoric" after failing to gain traction as a change agent along with Obama. Now her spin is that instead of change, Americans want solutions. How convenience is that? Hillary also is calling for <u>more debates</u> instead of more <u>speeches.</u> Actually, I think most of us prefer more speeches. Besides, a major role of the U.S. President is to inspire the nation. To achieve that goal, what better avenue is there than through speeches?

Sidebar: So let's recap. One potential leader doesn't think that we should have hope and one wants us to keep our hope in check. I'm sure there is logic there somewhere. I'm just having a hard time finding it.

Obama and McCain: Choices As Clear As Dawn and Dusk

Barack Obama and John McCain both won primaries tonight in Wisconsin, but that's where the similarities end. After his win, Obama gave an inspiring and substantive speech to a large group of voters in Houston, Texas. The crowd was energized and captivated. Obama's message was about the future.

After his victory, John McCain gave an uninspiring speech that received polite applause and referred to Obama with his message of hope, as an "empty suit." McCain continues to tie his hopes to the failed politics of the past seven years and actually seems to think that people prefer living in the past.

McCain and a lot of GOP talking heads want people to reject the notion that Obama is winning because America wants to solve its problems rooted in past protocols, past divisions, past partisan politics. Obama has communicated a vision of collaborative governance absent of wedge politics, race-based politics, left and right politics, red or blue states politics, but filled with United States politics.

Barack Obama has an inspiring message indeed and judging from the enthusiastic reception that Obama continues to receive, a lot of Americans are saying, I'm going to give this guy a try. And yet the opposition still insists that Americans do not want change and do not want progress and boldly implies that Americans cannot change.

Well, I truly do not know where the chips will eventually fall. However, if Obama wins the Democratic nomination and faces McClain in the general election, the choices will be crystal clear. If you embrace the possibilities of the future, then Obama is your dawn.

On the other hand, if you think that the best that America can do is live with a 51 to 49 percent majority and it's unfulfilled past, then McCain is your dusk.

The Problem with John McCain

John McCain arrogantly tells us that hope is a fabrication of our imagination. As I reflected on his stark reality about the future, numerous parallels came to mind.

McCain is the guy at work that when you want to try something new or do something differently is quick to say why change, we have always done things this way.

He is the guy who goes and returns the same way to work, to the store, on vacation, then wants to argue with you if you attempt to travel a different route. (Medical journals have recommended doing things differently to keep the brain functioning sharper).

He is the teacher or counselor that tells the young child to keep their aspirations in check because they could never expect to achieve such lofty goals. He is the one that doesn't need to be around the young and impressionable because he crushes dreams.

He is the guy who is quick to point out problems, but never offers a solution. He is the guy who fails by default, because he doesn't try.

He is the guy who sees the world through tunnel vision and wants everyone else to fit neatly within his narrowly drawn parameters.

Everyone has the right to choose their own line of thought however limited it may be, but this is never, never, never the person you want as your leader.

Sidebar: John McCain's idea of change is probably two dimes and a nickel in exchange for a quarter.

Tavis Still Clueless in New Orleans

Tavis Smiley still doesn't get it. In an interview today on XM Radio's P.O.T.U.S. 08, Smiley continued to insist that Barack Obama missed an opportunity by not attending Smiley's <u>summit</u> in New Orleans. Smiley also tried to discount the negative buzz directed towards him on the internet for acting like a jerk towards Obama, who respectfully refused his invitation to the summit due to a scheduling conflict in Texas.

Somehow, Tavis thinks that Obama has to be in New Orleans in order to talk to Black America. Well Tavis let me holla at you for a minute. We have TV, radio, newspapers and the internet. We have heard Obama speak to Black America. Obama spoke to Black America when he spoke to White America, Latino America, Italian America, and all America.

For too long, there has been too much division in this country. Although quite a few of us are cynics, we are hopeful that America can change for the better. That's why America is so captivated by Obama. Republicans wished for him. Now there is a good chance that they will get him. And to Obama's credit, some Republicans will defy polling trends and actually vote for him instead of against him.

There are many reasons to try and marginalize Obama. One reason might be that there will be a reduced need for bully pulpits...or bullies like Tavis.

Ralph Nader Should Stay in Hibernation

<u>He's back!</u> After messing things up in 2000, Ralph Nader who is a legend in his own mind resurfaces from the

depths of his dark and dreary den. I guess giving Florida to George Bush wasn't satisfaction enough.

I think that most people now know that a vote for Nader is like a vote not cast. If Nader had any real interest in becoming president, he would have run as a Democrat or a Republican. So as we are left scratching our heads yet again, we have to ask Nader, what is your real motivation?

Ralph, did you get an epiphany. The campaign has been underway for months. Did you have your head stuck in the sand? I guess having been <u>once</u> regarded as a respected consumer advocate wasn't the desired legacy. Now spoiler is more accurate. Please do the country a favor and return to your den and resume your hibernation.

Sidebar: "Hey Ralph... Smokey, Yogi, and Boo Boo miss your company."

Hillary Is a Sinking Ship

As an early Hillary Clinton supporter, I now feel that I owe Barack Obama an apology. I thought Hillary was the better candidate, thought Obama was too inexperienced and thought John Edwards had missed his opportunity.

Then as weeks and months passed, Obama got stronger and Hillary self-destructed. Hillary's skills apparently had been overestimated and Obama's skills underestimated. As Hillary's followed very expensive bad advice, Obama and his team proceeded to rewrite the book on how to run a winning campaign. I was wrong about Obama.

A few months ago, I posted an article to my weblog, LeadershipCultivation.com, which said Hillary could "<u>boost her positives.</u>" Today I am not as confident with that forecast. However, my best advice then and now is stay away from the <u>negative stuff,</u> because the strategy will backfire.

The strategy has backfired because Obama is simply a <u>phenomenal.</u> He has a date with destiny. I find myself relaxing my guard and trusting that some Republicans too are sincere about changing the tone in America. It's really time for the political civil wars to be over.

Barack and Hillary Are Both Very Good Candidates...But

The Democratic debate tonight only verified what a lot of Democrats and Republicans already know and that is Hillary Clinton and Barack Obama are both very good candidates who are running for President of the United States. To be truthful, they both were strong debaters. But beyond the basic traits which they possess, I think that Barack Obama has more intangibles.

The question now is who is the best leader? A leader at its core is someone who has followers and right now Obama has more followers. He has the gift to inspire and I perceive the ability to move persons to action. I commend him for staying on message of the need for a new model of change for the better and increased civility in handling the issues of today. I find that to be a ballot checking difference.

We all have problems with divorcing ourselves from the past. That's why we have the repeated and pointed references to <u>Farrakhan</u>, anti-Semitism, <u>African garb</u>, and the playful <u>mimicking</u> of someone delivering a speech who may actually believe the words which they communicate and who may actually believe that they can bring about change.

That ability to inspire is what makes folks of different races, political parties, core values and different cultures be willing to grasp the possibility that in our lifetime, we can move to a higher place.

Sidebar: If I were a preacher I think now would be an excellent time to inject the words, "Won't you come?"

Obama's Call for Change Will Require a Group Effort

Barack Obama has proven that he can take a punch and he looks more presidential day by day. He has shown great skill in being able to dodge or rebound from assaults by the Clinton Campaign that have shown that they are not above hitting below the belt. But it's the GOP, with their God-fearing Christian-rite (no, they are not right) that take gutter politics to a whole new level.

Now it is the Tennessee GOP and Ohio talk show host Bill Cunningham, who have brought to the forefront the GOP's sometimes bigoted tendencies in their attempt to smear and denigrate Obama. Their venomous behavior is un-Christ-like and I don't think that God is pleased.

Their diabolical behavior only validates the point made by Obama that change will not come easy. Too many low-crawlers are fueled by their self-absorbed meanness. But it's the people of all backgrounds that hope for positive change in the tenor of America, that must "denounce and reject" the perpetrators instead of remaining silent.

Sidebar: The power lies with the people.

CHAPTER 6 ~ March 2008

Clinton and Obama Campaigns: Experience vs. Judgment

Hillary Clinton likes to tout her <u>experience</u> and point to Barack Obama's perceived lack of <u>experience</u> as a key reason that she would be a better President of the United States. However, when we closely look at the <u>inept</u> way in which the Clinton presidential campaign has been run, we must conclude that in some instances, experience is highly overrated.

Hillary was the <u>presumptive</u> Democratic nominee. No one in the Democratic Party could touch her. So what does Hillary do at the first sign of trouble, she panicked. After her lost in Iowa, she acted irrationally when she quickly pulled the plug on her planned strategy or the lack thereof. That was a terrible decision.

The direction her campaign went from there was even more troubling. In the words of Dr. Martin Luther King, "[The Clinton Campaign] started doing some <u>nasty things</u>." In fact the things were so nasty and insulting that they alienated her majority support amongst Black voters who subsequently abandoned her in disgust. The result was Obama victories by wider margins than would have occurred otherwise. No doubt it was another terrible Clinton miscalculation.

When her anticipated winning margin of White and Latino voters didn't materialize, Hillary dismissed <u>Patti Solis Doyle</u>, her Latina campaign manager. Somebody had to take the fall for the dysfunctional strategy or again its lack thereof. The move <u>upset</u> some of her Latino supporters. Whatever happened to winning and losing as a team? Again, this was another example of bad decision making.

Now in fairness to Hillary, she didn't make all of the bad decisions by herself, but it was her exercise of judgment that put her team in place. So she is responsible for the results.

On the other hand, Obama, the "inexperienced" candidate, has done a superb job of running his campaign. He has exercised outstanding judgment. And when Obama was behind, he didn't panic. So is it judgment or experience, merit or tenure? Most companies will say that when they look to promote individuals, merit is a more important factor than tenure.

After an objective evaluation of the job performances of Hillary and Barack in running their presidential campaigns, a fair question is who is more deserving of being entrusted with executing the duties of the President of the United States?

Sidebar: In the Sixties, there was another young inexperienced man who gave great inspiration speeches and changed a nation. We now celebrate his birthday as a national holiday.

The Clinton Chameleon Campaign

Bill Clinton has said that Hillary is toast if she doesn't win both Texas and Ohio on March 4. Now, as Barack Obama has closed the huge gaps Hillary previously enjoyed in both states, the Clinton Campaign is hedging on its word. Currently, the Clinton spin is Obama should win both states and win both states by huge margins or it shows that he has lost momentum.

Sounds ridiculous? Well it's par for the course with the Clinton Campaign. The one consistency for them is that they have not been consistent. They change strategy so frequency in order to blend in with the flavor of the day, maybe Hillary should consider changing her last name to <u>chameleon</u>.

This fickle strategy has really gotten tired. If you don't plan to do it, then don't say it. But if you say it, like Nike, "just do it." This is yet one more example of the use of poor judgment on behalf of the Clinton campaign. So please stop flipping and please stop flopping.

Sidebar: As a chameleon, technically I guess you can lay claim to being a change agent.

Hillary Has Found Her Voice and It's Republican

After months of <u>chameleon-like</u> changes with her campaign strategies, Hillary Clinton has finally found her <u>true voice.</u> Surprise, surprise, it's Republican! With all the venom of <u>Karl Rove</u> or the late <u>Lee Atwater</u>, who to his credit sought forgiveness for his transgressions, Hillary has unleashed a barrage of <u>innuendos</u>, record <u>distortions</u>, <u>fear-mongering</u>, <u>race-baiting</u>, and flat out lies aimed towards Barack Obama, that would make most right-winged Republicans recoil.

Hillary isn't just using the <u>Republican playbook</u>; she's releasing her own edition. It's a win at any cost strategy that will surely cost Democratic Party unity in November. If Hillary benefits from her ill-advised tactics, in the fall a lot of people will have to decide which Republican candidate is more acceptable. Today in a vote between Hillary and John McCain, I choose McCain.

Right now for Democrats and voters at large, the choices couldn't be clearer. If we want more of the same old rhetoric, the same old Democratic/Republican partisanship, the same old Red State/Blue State nonsense, the same old class/race/religion divisiveness, the same old war, the same old Machiavellian Clintonism, which has revealed its true stripes with an air of entitlement, then vote for Hillary Clinton.

However, if we want civility in governance, like-minded <u>Republicans</u> and Democrats working together to find those real solutions that Hillary touts (because leadership does start at the top), if we want to unite the country and truly have a United States of America with its people working together instead of placing a dagger in each other's backs, if we want to achieve real change or at the least have the faith that real change can occur in our lifetime, since "Faith is the substance of things hoped for, the evidence of things not seen" (Heb.11:1), then vote for Barack Obama.

As the United States of America makes its choice for president, it might help to ponder these words from the <u>Robert Frost</u> poem, "The Road Not Taken", where

> "Two roads diverged in a wood, and I--
> I took the one less traveled by,
> And that has made all the difference."

Media Undermines Obama's Message of Hope

I have some beachfront property to sell. I really don't have any beachfront property, but what the heck it seems that a lot of folks are selling things these days that aren't real. And the mainstream media appears to be buying.

Barack Obama has had a couple of rough weeks. Through some shrew manipulation, Hillary Clinton has convinced the <u>media</u> to buy some beachfront property that doesn't exist. And Obama thinking that it might matter that the property doesn't exist, tried to tell somebody. But his words fell on deaf ears, since they were however, "just words." And everyone knows that words don't really matter. Right?

But Obama thinking that words still matter appears committed to telling people that the property doesn't exist because he feels that truth matters and the people need to know. But he has an uphill climb because the media seems intent on reporting about the marketing plan used to sell the beachfront property rather than reporting that the property doesn't exist.

Sidebar: Before I forget, I also have two front row tickets to the Final Four for sale at face value.

What Does GOP Rep. Steve King and Hillary Clinton Have in Common? ...Everything

Barack Obama is calling for change in the civility of American politics, but it appears that quite a few politicians see change as a hindrance to their self-serving agendas, namely getting elected at any cost.

Now GOP U.S. Rep. Steve King of Iowa while talking about radical Islamics, made some of the most egregious and radical statements ever made by an American politician in his attempt to discredit Obama. Why make the statements? King obvious feels that making bogus claims will help get him reelected and he also feels that the American people and the media will tolerate his bad boy behavior.

Switch to Hillary Clinton. In the days leading up to the Ohio and Texas primaries, Clinton made some of the most egregious and radical statements against Obama, even at one point seemingly endorsing John McCain, in a do or say anything all out attempt to win. Hillary made her claims with a straight face, surmising that a lot of Americans including the mainstream media will tolerate her bad girl behavior.

Witness this week Wolf Blitzer, of CNN, saying that Hillary has her mojo back completely ignoring the less than honorable methods her campaign used to try to discredit Obama. As long as the movie critics (the media) give Clinton raving reviews, it will be next to impossible for Obama to experience his hope of a <u>paradigm</u> shift in American politics. So what do Hillary Clinton and GOP U.S. Rep. Steve King have in common? In my opinion...*EVERYTHING*!

If Clinton Is the Nominee, Political Realignment Will Occur

Give the Clintons credit for sticking with a plan. In her quest for the White House, Hillary encountered an unexpectedly strong challenge from Barack Obama which threatened her plans of becoming the Democratic nominee.

To counter, after Obama's win in Iowa the Clintons proceeded to "<u>blacken him up</u>" to create a Black vs. White contest. It appeared to work in New Hampshire. The Clintons showing a lack of confidence in keeping their almost 50/50 Black voter support, activated a plan to get winning margins of White and Latino voters. The plan counted on a future recovery of a portion of Black support in the general election. More will be shared about that later.

Black voters initially gave the Clintons the benefit of doubt until Bill's <u>race-baiting</u> reference of Rev. Jesse Jackson after Obama's win in South Carolina. Given their past unwavering support of the Clintons, Black voters became disgusted with their behavior. To Black voters, the Clintons had earned a level of contempt once reserved for right-wingers like Jesse Helms.

Fast-forward to the present. The Clintons have officially activated their recovery phase of lost Black voter support. That's why we have Hillary, Bill and <u>Ed Rendell</u>, the governor of Pennsylvania <u>dropping hints</u> of Obama as the Clintons choice for Vice President to promote a win-win situation. The comments are correctly seen as attempts to marginalize Obama support in upcoming primaries. Some gullible <u>media</u> types hail the comments as Clinton good faith gestures.

But here's the Clinton reality. The Clintons know that if their <u>unscrupulous</u> campaign against Obama is successful; their only hope for victory in November is with Obama on the ticket as VP. No big price to pay for a victory. With Bill around, it won't matter who the VP is anyway. However, if Obama refuses the request, the exodus of Obama supporters to John McCain, especially Black voters, will be unprecedented. McCain will cruise to the White House and ruin a "perfect Clinton plan." Those poll numbers of Clinton vs. McCain will be meaningless. It's not the type of real <u>change</u> that Obama envisions, but political alignments would change nonetheless.

Sidebar: Too bad there won't be any governor contests in Pennsylvania and Ohio.

Democratic Primary Process Needs a Revamp

The political mess in Florida and Michigan has highlighted the imperfect Democratic Presidential Primary system in much the same manner as the Florida debacle of 2000 highlighted problems with the Electoral College. It would take a U.S. Constitutional Amendment to change the Electoral College, but a change to the Democratic primary system is achievable.

For this year, the existing rules must be adhered to by Florida and Michigan. We can't change the rules after the game starts in order to gain an advantage. Florida and Michigan did not follow the rules. They must not be allowed at this point to declare Hillary as the winner because that would not be fair to Barack Obama or any of the other candidates. However, I do share the states' motivation for wanting to conduct their primaries earlier. It is not a fair process for Iowa and New Hampshire to always conduct the first vetting of the candidates.

Since it would not be feasible to conduct all the primaries on the same date, states should take turns in a rotational system that determines when primaries could be held. For example, if Iowa and New Hampshire are first in 2008, they would be last in 2012.

That's a change that does not require changing the U.S. Constitution and it would make the country feel more like equal partners in the selection of the Democratic nominee. And all of us would welcome a more fair and equitable selection process, wouldn't we?

Thank You Donna Brazile!

<u>Hillary Clinton</u> appears to want a race war! <u>Ed Rendell</u> appears to want a race war! <u>Geraldine Ferraro</u> appears to want a race war! <u>CNN</u> pundits appear to want to promote a race war! Thank you Donna Brazile for pulling the CNN talking points out of the gutter.

This contest started out being about change. But for some, change can be a losing proposition. Here you have <u>Barack Obama</u> trying to appeal to people of all races, religions, economic status, in big states, in little states, in the United States and what do we end up with, CNN talking about the little picture. Hillary, Ed, Geraldine, CNN all talking about the divisions of race. Coincidental? I don't think so. Some folks see that as a winning formula. Old habits are proving hard to break. America, rise up. The Civil War is over!

Sidebar: America, welcome to the crossroads. Choose wisely.

Hillary's Plan of Selfish Deception

Hillary knows she can't win the 2008 Democratic Nomination. But she thinks that she can win a race war. From the moment that her chances of winning began to dim, Hillary said to hell with change and forward thinking and activated a plan of White people to the left and Black people to the right. And if that plan doesn't work, oh well, there's always 2012.

Hillary insults the intelligence of objective and clear thinking Americans with her claim that Bill Clinton, Ed Rendell, and now Geraldine Ferraro orchestrated injection of racial politics into her contest with Barack Obama is not a cold and calculating plan by her campaign to sabotage Obama's and the Democrats' chances in November.

Hillary is using a gold-toed roachkiller strategy where the thought process is I don't mind screwing myself if the outcome is that I screw you also. That's a small price to pay if I can extract some of personal satisfaction. It appears that Hillary's anger at Obama for not "waiting his turn" cuts to the bone.

My only question is when will the Democratic Party leadership step in and restore order. Right now Hillary is on a mission of slash and burn that will cripple the Democratic Party for years to come. Talk about sour grapes!

Sidebar: I think that even Machiavelli is now shaking his head in disgust.

Keith Olbermann Uncovers Path to Democratic Party Leadership's Backbone

Hillary Clinton has gone unchecked for months by the Democratic Party as she blazed a trail of self-destruction for the Democratic Party and herself.

Now Keith Olbermann, by calling Hillary out, has thrown the Democratic Leadership and superdelegates a lifeline. How the Democratic Party and superdelegates choose to use it may determine the future of the Democratic Party.

Given the mischief that has taken place, we are left to ponder if this is what God meant when he said, "For we wrestle not against flesh and blood, but against principalities, against powers, against the rulers of the darkness of this world, against spiritual wickedness in high places." Eph.6:12.

There is a constant battle being waged inside of us between right and wrong, good and evil. Albeit in the short-term, it appears that evil is winning. I say that with a caveat, because the promise is that eventually, "[we also reap what we sow]." Gal. 6:7-8.

Barack Obama: Actions More Like Rev. Wright or More Like Christ?

May the words of my mouth and the meditations of my heart be acceptable in Your sight oh Lord my God and my Redeemer. I attend church on a regular basis, but observe that I didn't ask for the acceptance of my preacher or a preacher anywhere. The preacher may be the spiritual leader of my congregation, but Christ is the Head of the Christian Church. Living the life of a Christian is an independent choice. I think a popular Christian song says it best, "Though none go with me, I still will follow."

As I was watching Anderson Cooper on CNN tonight, I was struck by a comment that guest Tony Perkins made when he said that "[he didn't see how Barack Obama could attend church sermons preached by Rev. Dr. Jeremiah Wright and not be adversely influenced by them]." Well, the correct answer is "easily." God gives us a discerning spirit and a Bible to research and verify that what the preacher says is truly the Word of God. Everything the preacher says is not taken at face value. And Mr. Perkins as a professed Christian, I'm sure that you are familiar with the Biblical command "study to show yourself approved."

If you want to know if Barack Obama is influenced more by Rev. Wright or Jesus Christ, you ask him. Then you take him at his word. The real measure of a person's sincerity is who the person emulates. In the case of Obama, do his actions more closely reflect the sound bite sermon of Rev. Wright or do his actions try to emulate the teachings of Christ?

Christ is a unifier. He accepts people equally regardless of their earthly status. Isn't that what Obama has sought to do when he called upon Democrats, Republicans, Black people, White people, Latino people, young people and old people, men and women, to work together for the betterment of America. No other candidate has captured the imagination of the country and inspired the nation more by their message of hope and call for change than Barack Obama.

But why do some people work so hard to keep the status quo. An old wise man once said that some people just like to wallow in mess. Why? An obvious reason is that positive change could dry up their gravy train. What would Rush Limbaugh do if his audience suddenly stopped listening to his nonsense? Even when in our hearts we know that this country could use a makeover, we still resist. Another reason for our hesitation could be that we know that the journey will be difficult and the path of least resistance looks more inviting.

However, the question remains. As we have observed Barack Obama over these many months, has he exhibited behavior more like Rev. Wright (as seen in the

YouTube video) or behavior more closely resembling the teachings of Christ? I think the answer is clear. Barack Obama has revealed himself as someone that Americans could be proud to call their President and I hope he gets a little Heavenly intervention.

Barack Obama and Racial Scar Tissue

This morning as I drove to work, I had the pleasure of listening to an inspirational spot on the radio by a nationally renowned local minister, David Chadwick, who said that "[to hope or despair is a choice]" and he also said that "[we have the freedom to decide if we are going to have hope or despair]."

Then around noon, I had the displeasure of listening to the caustic and calculating Rush Limbaugh trying to marginalize Barack Obama after his speech about race relations in America, by saying that Obama had "[wanted to transcend race, but is now the candidate of race]." I also listened to his tag line which boasted, "Rush Limbaugh, the man who runs America" and felt that a more accurate and honest tag line would be, Rush Limbaugh, the man who wants to run America into the ground.

In the afternoon in Charlotte, I got the opportunity to attend a Town Hall Meeting with Barack Obama. During his familiar stump speech about changing America, Obama talked about the need to "[get past divisions based on race and religion]" and acknowledged that "the status quo will resist change." He also said that change will not be easy, but will "have to happen from the bottom up." It will have to happen from the bottom up, meaning we the people have to be the catalysts for change. Obama also made another interesting observation that it will take young folks getting more involved to make that revolutionary transformation.

Why the young people? I think it's because older people have too much racial scar tissue. I get amused when I hear people ask, "How could Rev. Wright say the things he said and not be anti-American and why didn't Obama leave the congregation?" Give Mike Huckabee credit for acknowledging that America hasn't always been good to Black Americans and there is some residual scar tissue from old wounds that some ultra conservative talk show hosts and overly-ambitious politicians sometimes intentionally intensify. To answer the second question, parishioners are able to extract the Word of God from the messenger and Barack probably would have left the congregation if he like so many others had harbored a long existing desire to be president. His decision to stay would say that he didn't and supports his claim that he "[hasn't been thinking about running for president since kindergarten]."

Now Barack Obama has America talking about race and Rev. Wright has people wondering whether he is anti-American because of his sometime inclusion of inflammatory language in his sermons. Well, I think that Rev. Wright can love his country even if he reveals his personal scar tissue. It's very similar to the ability to love a person, but hate their behavior. And if we are honest with ourselves, a lot of us have relationships like that in our backgrounds.

Shortly after beginning seventh grade, my family moved away from a small North Carolina town to a larger town with the hope of finding better living conditions. I left behind segregated schools, restrooms, water fountains and movie theaters where black people were required to sit in the balcony to view a movie. Before I was enrolled in a mostly white school, my opinion of White people had been formed from TV news showing White people bombing churches killing little Black girls or using baseball bats to keep Black children from attending their schools. For good measure, throw in lynchings, cross burnings, police with dogs, water hoses, and an unfair judicial system, I thought I had all the information I needed.

My teachers and classmates were all White and the school was located in a White neighborhood. My homeroom, math and art teachers treated me kindly, but my music teacher was harsh and once had the class serenade me with a rendition of "Mammy's Little Baby Loves Shortening Bread." My young classmates were generally friendly and I fought or wrestled with some of the guys everyday on the playground.

One day during our lunch break, my playmates and I left the schoolyard and went to a neighborhood snack bar to get something to eat. Although this wasn't our first time there, on this occasion the owner approached us and said of me "I ain't got nothing against you, but some of my customers don't want you eating in the same room; you can stay but eat in the back." I was hurt and angry. But the thing that happened next affected my life more than the racial prejudice of some grownups.

That day, my friends Ted and Nick, courageously stood in contempt and said "Let's leave; we don't have to eat here." I will never forget how Ted and Nick stood up for me even though I received racial scars. If I were a preacher trying to give theological meaning to the events of that day, it would be "[the white men] meant it for evil, but God meant it for good." A sound bite centered on just my feelings about the white men in that snack bar could convey the wrong message.

However, in proper context, the actions of Ted and Nick made me aware that all White people weren't bad. I learned at an early age that good or evil is an individual choice. And the closing part of that message is to "love your neighbor as God has loved you, even when they despitefully use you."

I think that Barack Obama was able to attend Trinity United for twenty years because he heard the contextual messages. When you listen carefully to Mr. Obama you will hear a <u>message</u> that challenges us to turn from our sometimes tainted past and strive for positive change unimpeded by racial, religious or political divisions.

Mainstream Media Risks Becoming Marginalized

Remember when retired CBS Evening News Anchor, <u>Walter Cronkite</u> would say "And that's the way it is" and you trusted his reporting enough to believe him. Remember when Cronkite and other reporters tried to actually "report" the news instead of making or "influencing" what ended up being news. We know Fox News can't be trusted. Fox News long ago marginalized itself when it became little more than a video version of the Rush Limbaugh Show.

Occasionally, I tune to Fox News just to see what new scheme the mischief makers have cooked up. Picture this panel of objectivity, Brit Hume, Fred Barnes, Charles Krauthammer and Juan Williams sitting around stoking the flames of divisiveness with their "commentary" that Barack Obama hasn't explained enough to <u>their</u> satisfaction his relationship with Rev. Jeremiah Wright. And isn't that Chris Wallace "Countdown until Barack Obama appears on FOX News" really silly and adolescent?

Although bias reporting is the expectation from FOX, in some ways CNN and MSNBC are just as bad. Maybe there is merit to the claim that CNN has become synonymous with "Clinton News Network." CNN and MSNBC continue to run the same sound bite video clips of Rev. Wright taken out of context while refusing to get off their journalistic behinds to explore other portions of the videos that might give more insight into the overall message that Rev. Wright was attempting to convey. During one of his "inflammatory" sermons, Rev. Wright incidentally had words of praise for Bill Clinton. Here's a novel idea, do an inside report about the different methods that Black preachers use to reach their parishioners. Plainspoken sermons are commonplace in the Black Church, but they conclude with love your neighbor as God has loved you.

On a more positive note, I do applaud David Gergen, Roland Martin, Candy Crawley, Jack Cafferty, and Keith Olbermann for at least trying to do objective and analytical reporting. At least from them we don't get the usual, "he made this gain...but", hogwash. I also applaud the blogs. Without Talking Points Memo, The Huffington Post, Politico.com and other similar sites, we wouldn't have gotten the Rev. Wright photo with Bill Clinton taken at his Monica Lewinsky repentance prayer breakfast or more insight into Rev. Wright beyond the sound bites.

Nevertheless, it's still a sad commentary when we can't trust the mainstream media to maintain the journalistic standard set by Cronkite, Ed Bradley and Ted Koppel. I hope that mainstream media does some soul searching before it becomes totally irrelevant. The Society of Professional Journalists has developed an outstanding code of ethics for journalists. Talking heads should review it more often.

Obama Faces High Noon, How Will the People Respond?

Some of you may have seen the western classic, "High Noon", which starred actor Gary Cooper as a town marshal forced to face a band of outlaws alone because the local town folks were too afraid to help him fight for a just cause. Carl Foreman, the screenwriter, said "the film was intended as an allegory of the contemporary failure of intellectuals to combat the rise of <u>McCarthyism</u>, as well as how people in Hollywood had remained silent while their peers were blacklisted." Sound familiar?

<u>Barack Obama</u>, the candidate of change and the candidate who wants America to have an adult discussion about <u>race relations</u>, now faces a challenge similar to that of the marshal in "High Noon." Like it or not, there exist some deep-rooted racial prejudices, racial insensitivities, and racial distrust that prevent the United States from achieving greater success even as the rest of the world looks to us as an utopia. We still have some self-improvement to perform around our own front doors.

Last week, when Obama spoke in Charlotte, his <u>acknowledgment</u> that "[change will be difficult...that the challenge will come from the power brokers...and he couldn't make change happen alone]" has not escaped me. I guess that's why I thought about "High Noon." When needed, the good citizens couldn't find the courage to stand up for righteousness. They refused a call to action even when their well-being and self-respect were on the line and instead took a cowardly exit.

I have watched with amazement and frustration while some members of the traditional mainstream media have acted like a gang of outlaws by serving as the <u>chief barrier</u> to Barack Obama being able to engage fellow Americans in a serious discussion about race. This media has bombarded us with sensationalized YouTube snippets of Rev. Jeremiah Wright sermons taken out of context. They have insisted on being chief antagonists when the country could benefit from a comprehensive examination of the Black church and the cultural differences that influence Black ministers to preach sermons in a manner that some White people might regard as offensive.

My request for the media is to conduct comprehensive reporting and trust the people to be able to make up their own minds absent of media advocacy for one position over another. That has not happened with any degree of regularity. Instead the media have collectively acted like political combatants with the goal of defeating Obama in his quest to bring real change to America. I earlier wrote that mainstream media need to revisit their journalistic code of ethics because they are doing the public a great disservice.

High noon is approaching and it's time to organize a posse to help Obama face the gang of outlaws. Going forward, when members of the mainstream media refuse to engage in objective discourse about race and deliberately seek to discredit Obama or any other candidate with innuendo or unnecessary badgering, make note of their advertisers during that portion of the "news" and formally contact the advertisers and media CEOs to voice displeasure.

We are part of the same posse and may indeed need to head the enemy off at the pass. When you read my paraphrased version of the Thomas Shepherd Hymn, "Must Jesus Bear the Cross Alone", what will be your answer?

"[Must Obama bear the racial problem alone
And all of America go free?
No, there's a role in this discussion for everyone,
And there's a role for you and me.]"

CHAPTER 7 ~ April 2008

Bill and Hillary Clinton: Two Out of 303,774,752

Today, Bill and Hillary Clinton are 2 persons out of a growing U.S. population of 303,774,752. While most persons will never ascend to the U.S. presidency, the Clinton household has been fortunate enough to produce one U.S. President. Also, judging from their actions during this Democratic primary season, I get the feeling that they are hell bent on producing two U.S Presidents.

It may be time to limit American households to producing no more than one president. Whereas Bush One entered the White House with a deep resume and did a respectable job, we all know that Bush Two struggled. Do we really want to find out how a Clinton Two would perform?

After we place term limits on households, consider placing limits on the number of spokespersons assigned to one campaign. Aren't you tired of Mark Penn, Harold Ickes, James Carville, Paul Begala, Phil Singer, Howard Wolfson, etc. etc. etc.? Which one is the chief strategist, anyway?

More Mess for Obama from Clinton and McCain

In this never ending political season, there is yet another attempt by Hillary Clinton and John McCain to marginalize Barack Obama in order to weaken his presidential candidacy. Obama's comments, "When you're bitter, you turn to what you can count on", made in reference to some small town voters, were true. But of course we can't have frank discussions in this country without parts of the conversation being taken out of context and showing up in a political sound bite.

Well leave it to Hillary to try to turn a flicker into a flame to sway superdelegates to overturn the will of the people. Hillary insists that this latest controversy will hurt Obama in the general election and her <u>surrogates</u> are just getting warmed up. Add this latest one to all the other none issues designed to weaken Obama in November. Right now, goal number one is to get the news media to pick the story up and run with it. Their strategy appears to be working at least in the short term on CNN and XM Radio P.O.T.U.S. 08. Now if we can just get these media types to <u>report the news</u> instead of trying to influence what is newsworthy.

Of course I hope that superdelegates have discerned that no matter what trickery Hillary employs to cast doubt on Obama, that she will never be accepted as the nominee if she benefits from her deceptive political tactics. That scenario is more certain to guarantee a Republican victory in November than any comments by Obama taken out of context. The Republicans will also have a hard time convincing anyone that they are more concerned about everyday citizens. The Republicans are the party of the real elitists as evidenced by their well documented policies. Given Hillary's <u>propensity to embrace</u> what used to uniquely be Republican strategies and McCain's decades of experience as a Republican, I think that they would have the most trouble looking out for the interests of middle America.

Obama is not a career politician and has skillfully adjusted to his political hiccups. You can bet that Hillary and McCain no longer underestimate him. However, Obama has learned one more lesson. That lesson is to beware of "sleeper" donors like the one in San Francisco who can surface at any moment.

Barack Obama: The Ultimate Insider

Newsflash! Barack Obama is half Black and half White. If Obama harbors this bias against White people that some folks claim, wouldn't he be the first to know? Wouldn't he risk internal conflict between his Black and White sides? Since Obama can't hide his feelings from himself, shouldn't we trust him to have everyone's interests at heart? So until we witness some outward sign of an internal battle being waged, shouldn't we just follow Rep. Jim Clyburn's advice and "chill out" with this silly Obama disrespects working-class White America silliness?

The Revenge-Seeking Wrath of Rev. Wright

The 2008 Presidential Campaign has discredited more than its share of commonly held beliefs. Before this campaign, it was widely held that overly negative politics filled with innuendos, inaccuracies, distortions, racial overtones and flat out lies were exclusive to Karl Rove and the Republican Party. That was before we witnessed the campaign tactics that the Hillary Clinton campaign used against Barack Obama.

Then there was the "gold-toed roach killer syndrome" which I erroneously thought was largely unique to southern White voters. It's where White voters so motivated by prejudices against Black people would support political strategies that equally harmed their own race because of the joy they get from sticking it to Black people.

I used to think that hell-bent on destruction tactics also were unique to Republicans. I have been educated. Rev. Jeremiah Wright with the stated motivation of defending the Black Church is running a self-serving campaign to destroy the presidential candidacy of Barack Obama. Rev. Wright appears bitter and is displaying some characteristics that run counter to Christian principles. He wants revenge, but the Bible teaches us that "revenge is mine says the Lord." The Bible also tells us that "we must decrease so that God can increase."

So what has Rev. Wright done? He participated in a Pharisees and Publican-like campaign of praying in the public square with his high profile appearances on PBS, at the Detroit NAACP Convention, and at the National Press Club. Again, I think the Biblical response to this type of self-promotion, is that it's not to please God, but to instead find reward amongst men.

Now for all the pundits who have asked the question about the influence of Rev. Wright on Barack Obama, I think you have your answer. Barack Obama, actions more like Rev. Jeremiah Wright or more like Jesus? Rev. Wright shows us why we should always follow God instead of putting our trust in mankind. I think Obama understands this basic Christian principle. Give any human being enough time and they will eventual fail you. Why? Humans aren't perfect. Only Christ holds that unique status.

Well Rev. Wright has built some provocative speed bumps along the crossroads to change, but the destinations points remain unchanged. Do we want real change or do we want to continue with the same old divisiveness of 51% to 49% politics? Do we want the constant gridlock between people who refuse to find common ground that would benefit the common good? I'm reminded again that Robert Frost asked the same type of question with his thought provoking words. "Two roads diverged in a wood, and I--I took the one less traveled by…."

Which road will America take? That's a decision that shouldn't be influenced by the actions of Rev. Wright. I think Barack Obama was strong enough to choose the road less traveled. He shouldn't have to make the journey alone.

CHAPTER 8 ~ May 2008

CNN's Donna Brazile Tears GOP Strategist Alex Castellanos a New One

Just when all confidence in the <u>mainstream media</u> to be committed to reporting the news instead of spinning the news was about to dissipate, Donna Brazile <u>once again</u> stepped up and said stop the bull crap. Tonight as GOP strategist Alex Castellanos, invoked the names of William Ayers and Jeremiah Wright completely out of context, in an obvious attempt to cast aspersions upon Barack Obama, Donna Brazile forcefully stepped in and tore Alex a new one.

Donna also took CNN host, Campbell Brown, Paul Begala and Lanny Davis to task. Campbell tried to imply that the only reason Brazile was being so forceful was because Brazile was supporting Obama, but Brazile held her ground. Brazile also neutralized attempts by Clinton supporters Begala and Davis to spin distortions. Begala and Davis were at a loss for words.

Finally with Wolf Blitzer nervously anticipating Obama overtaking Clinton in Indiana, the next sour grapes came from Mayor Tom McDermott of Hammond, Indiana, a Clinton supporter. McDermott implied that Mayor Rudy Clay of Gary, Indiana, an Obama supporter, was engaged in hanky panky because the vote from Lake County was slow in being reported. It appeared that McDermott's real motivation was to spin a story about Hillary Clinton winning Indiana, which McDermott did in an awkward manner once the votes came in. I think Mayor McDermott owes Mayor Clay an apology. What a cad!

Once again, thank you Donna Brazile for telling your colleagues to stop the bull crap. Now maybe we can get back to talking about the issues. And thank you

North Carolina for being a game changer! How about it Wolf? Can we get you to write a story about Barack Obama getting his mojo back?

Barack Obama Refuels His Mojo

I had hoped that Wolf Blitzer of CNN would have beaten me to the punch and written about how Barack Obama had gotten his mojo back in a manner similarly to what he once wrote about <u>Hillary Clinton.</u> I decided I couldn't wait on Wolf any longer.

After his huge and game changing victory in North Carolina, Barack Obama has refueled his mojo. On Tuesday night, Obama made the most inspiring and energetic speech that he had made in weeks. It personally made me flashback to the moment that this <u>former Hillary Clinton supporter,</u> first leaped aboard the Obama Express. And didn't Obama look and sound presidential?

Barack was back doing what Barack does best. He inspires people to do great things. As Obama spoke, I saw a crowd that appeared to move mentally and spiritually inside the realm of possibilities that Obama so eloquently painted for them. It is truly amazing and gratifying to think that America could move to a higher plain. It's a higher plain where there is less political strife and more collaboration for the common good. It's a higher plain where people actually want to live together in peace and harmony. A higher plain where we as Americans care more about each other and come together to solve complex problems regardless of race, religion, political party affiliation, or economic status.

With Obama, we see that plateau as a possibility that we can experience and we want that experience for our children. For too long, we have been running in place, but Obama represents real change. Obama has all the candidates talking about change because they see it as good politics given the connection Obama has made with the American people.

Obama again reminded us that change will not come easy. As mutually beneficial it would be to rid the United States of divisiveness, racial tensions, and political gridlock, too many people continue to work overtime to hold onto the status quo. Just today, Clinton who has fallen even farther behind in the race for the Democratic nomination erroneously stated that White people will <u>not vote</u> for Obama in big enough numbers. To paraphrase the late <u>Senator Lloyd Bentsen</u>, "I know White people and that is simply not the truth."

You have to wonder about Hillary's real motivation. Surely she must know that the superdelegates will not give her the nomination after proving that she can't beat Obama in a fair fight. So what's her angle? Is it to weaken Obama so that he will lose in the general election against McCain and put herself in position to run again in 2012? Or is it a selfish <u>gold-toed roachkiller</u> tactic to make sure that Obama, who refused to "wait his turn", loses the race for the presidency at any cost in order to give the Clintons some measure of personal satisfaction?

Despite having Hillary as a constant distraction, I am so glad to see Obama get back to doing the things that made him a <u>phenomenon</u>. He makes us believe that positive change actually can take place. And even when the masses fail to sufficiently support him, Obama is proving to us that he is not afraid to keep trying. That is a noble quality. So even as some continue to promote divisions and as the mainstream media can't seem to find its way, I still believe that Obama has been chosen at this time and place to <u>lead</u> America to greater heights. It appears that voters in North Carolina and Indiana agree.

Barack Obama and Hillary Clinton Together...Maybe

When Tim Kaine, Bill Richardson, Bob Casey and now John Edwards all endorsed Barack Obama for president, and stood together shoulder to shoulder with Barack smiling and waving to the crowds, each pairing looked good! And they all gave enthusiastic endorsement speeches. If Richardson had been as energetic during his own campaign as he was for Barack, his candidacy may have lasted longer. Now the spotlight turns to Hillary Clinton.

As a former Hillary Clinton underlinesupporter, I moved away from her when she abandoned her positive attributes. As someone who looks for the positive traits in people regardless of race, color, creed, religion, gender, I was deeply defended. In a nutshell, I felt like a jilted voter. You may know the feeling. When someone you love does you wrong, despite hurt feelings, you still try to hold on to the relationship. But as hard as you try, the person you once loved, slowly can become an object of contempt. That's especially true when that person continues to engage in the conduct that created the disappointment in the first place. If you don't comprehend the feelings I'm trying to explain, then find and listen to one of my favorite songs, "By the Time I Get to Phoenix." Both Glen Campbell and Isaac Hayes have excellent versions that teach about disappointment.

To continue the story, sometimes after escaping a bad relationship, you find a better good one. That's what happened when I listened to Barack Obama with a mind clear of Hillary. It was an amazing moment. Obama's speech after a primary victories, sold me on his positive vision for America. Who wouldn't love the idea of no more Washington gridlock, no more antagonistic divisiveness, no more red state/blue state nonsense, but a United States of America. Some people called his vision just words, but great leaders inspire with words. Obama's words fill me with hope and there is no turning back.

Now return with me to Hillary. Would she be good running mate for Barack Obama? Well some of her supporters and surrogates sure seem to think so. I think Hillary realized some time ago that she can't win the nomination and began jockeying for the VP slot. In a way Hillary is the Obama opposite. Like it or not, Hillary represents much of what we despise about the politics of old that we need to reject in order to elevate this country. Obama clearly represents the future.

Before Obama puts Clinton on the ticket he should consider the fit. Could he trust her? Alex Castellanos, a GOP political pundit, joked on CNN that ["Obama would have to have a food taster"] if he put Hillary on the ticket. I want to think that he is wrong. So I will withhold final judgment until the moment comes when Hillary endorses Obama for the presidency and they stand on the podium embraced together and waving to the crowd with a promise of working together to restore America to greatness. Obama said it wouldn't be easy to bring about real change. No kidding. There would be this requirement for Hillary to be selected as Veep. Without compromise, I would insist there be no reference to "this is the way we used to do things" and that Hillary comes minus her chief political strategists Howard Wolfson and Lanny Davis. The jury is still out on Terry McAuliffe, Paul Begala, and the biggest wild card of all, former President Bill Clinton.

The Reason Why I Admire Donna Brazile

After sitting patiently through all the arguments back and forth about whether the Michigan election was flawed or a legitimate election, the woman whom I admire more and more each day, cut to the chase. Donna Brazile said her mother always told her that ["If you change the rules in the middle of the game or if you change the rules at the end of the game, it's referred to as cheating"].

So whether it's a game of spades, horseshoes, or checkers, the same principle should apply when determining the best solution for Michigan, don't tolerate cheating. So Donna Brazile, I applaud you for continuing to be unafraid to say that the emperor is not wearing any clothes even as others validate such nonsense with their silent.

CHAPTER 9 ~ June 2008

Hillary, One Leader at a Time, Please!

Congratulations to Barack Obama, the 2008 Democratic Presidential Nominee! It was exciting to watch and listen to Barack as he made an inspiring speech to a very excited crowd. I listened to the speech on MSNBC to escape hearing yet another irritating commentary by <u>Wolf Blitzer</u> on CNN.

Hillary Clinton, after being introduced as the "next president of the United States", made a self-serving speech to promote her quest to get the vice-presidential slot. After hearing her speech tonight, I feel compelled to retract the suggestion I put forth yesterday that Hillary might be able to work as Obama's VP. I am now convinced to the contrary. Hillary is much too stubborn to ever accept a subordinate role to Obama as her commander-in-chief.

So despite the insistence or suggestion by her supporters that Obama put Hillary on the ticket, naming Hillary as VP would be Obama's first bad decision as the nominee. The VP should be your partner, not your chief antagonist. A major challenge to any leader is to have an ambitious associate who constantly promotes their own agenda ahead of the agenda established by the authorized leader.

My suggestion to Hillary is to find someplace else other than the VP slot to exercise leadership skills. As the immortals would say on the Highlander TV series, "There can be only one." In a similar fashion, there can only be one president in an Obama White House. Anything else would be a formula for disaster!

Wes Clark Is Barack Obama's Best Choice for VP

I like General Wesley Clark and he would be a great compliment to Barack Obama as vice president. Why Wes Clark? He has all the needed credentials. Clark graduated at the top of his class at West Point and was a Rhodes Scholar. He has elderly statesmen-like qualities having served as a Four-Star General and NATO Supreme Allied Commander where he commanded troops during the Kosovo War with no loss of U.S. lives.

Clark has a Jewish heritage, was a Hillary Clinton supporter (who didn't go overboard), served as a military advisor, is businessman, and has Southern roots with moderate political views. What more could you ask for in a vice presidential candidate? Clark adds value to an Obama ticket.

As he recently showed on MSNBC, General Clark definitely has the stature to go head to head with John McCain on foreign policy. If I'm looking for advice on foreign policy, with no disrespect of McCain, I would listen to the brilliant General who directed a major military campaign. We know that McCain suffered as a POW, but Clark also suffered four gunshot wounds while serving in Vietnam.

There are a lot of outstanding persons that Obama can choose as a running mate. Since another favorite Mark Warner is out of the picture, Wes Clark is definitely my current choice for the slot. And Obama/Clark has a nice ring to it.

CHAPTER 10 ~ July 2008

Lou Dobb Negatively Spins Obama's Suggestion to Learn Spanish

When I lived in Germany, my German and British friends jokingly baited me with three questions. What do you call someone who speaks three languages? What do you call someone who speaks two languages? And what do you call someone who speaks one language? The answers in order were trilingual if you spoke three languages, bilingual if your spoke two and American if you spoke one. My friends enjoyed a good laugh at my expense.

Well tonight on the CNN Newsroom, regular Barack Obama basher Lou Dobbs, attempted to spin Barack Obama's recent comments that "American kids needed to learn how to speak <u>Spanish</u>" into a negative. Dobbs sarcastically opined that Obama's suggestion was elitist and patronizing especially to the American "working class."

For reasons unknown, political pundits and some members of the mainstream media like Dobbs really are the ones who with regularity are guilty of patronizing and insulting the intelligence of the American working class. It's as if Dobbs and other <u>detractors</u> from honest dialogue think that working class Americans, presumably dominated by blue collar workers, lack the capacity to understand that a lifestyle improvement such as learning a different language would also provide benefits to them as it does to Americans in general.

Dobbs skipped over the fact that Obama also advocated that immigrants to America needed to learn how to speak English. When I lived in Europe, I observed that a lot of Europeans spoke English in addition to their native language. It was a common expectation that Americans had of our European hosts. It was in Europe also that I became familiar with ethnocentrism that when applied to Americans, means that we have the tendency to elevate the importance of our values above those of people from other places.

So in a nutshell, Lou Dobbs is wrong. When he gets back on his immigration soapbox and attempts to turn Obama's comments about learning another language into a wedge issue, I hope the American working class are smarter and more perceptive than Dobbs appears to give them credit.

President Barack Obama Will Face Unrealistic Expectations

Many of us have long been frustrated by American political strategies which have nothing to do with serving the people and everything to do with preserving special interests. So when the inspirational Barack Obama came along and offered to end our frustrations with "change that we can believe in", we enthusiastically jumped on the bandwagon. In fact, so many of us jumped and even pushed the wagon when necessary, that Obama is now the presumptive Democratic nominee for president of these United States of America. However Obama is rapidly becoming more acquainted with the meaning of the common cliché "stuck between a rock and a hard place" due to unrealistic expectations which he now faces from some of his most ardent supporters.

Recently, Obama received uncharacteristic criticism for reasons which Rev. Jesse Jackson has famously referred to as "Barack talking down to Black people", for his public yet accurate assertion that some Black men need to take more responsibility to ensure the success of their families. Call this reaction to Obama cognitive dissonance, but these are two examples of potential problems that lie ahead for Obama when he makes decisions that he deems to be in the best interest of the country.

Special interests are not unique to one group or cause. I have special interests and you have special interests and invariably my special interests have the potential to conflict with yours. That is when compromise is required. In governance, compromise and gridlock cannot occupy the same space. For the United States to have a realistic chance of emerging from partisan gridlock that has stunted its growth, a successful leader will have to govern using both collaboration and compromise.

That is a reality that Obama understands judging by his recent decisions. To his credit, Obama has tried to communicate that changing the political landscape will require both give and take. Maybe Obama would have been more effective in getting this point across if he had asked his audiences the same question that my Pastor often asks when he wants to increase the retention level of his congregants. That question is "Are you listening?"

Assuming that you were not listening closely, Barack Obama has repeatedly emphasized that he is running to be President of the United States of America. By definition that includes being president of red states and blue states, Liberals and Conservatives, Republicans and Democrats. Fill in the blanks with your special interests and Barack has got you covered. However in the interest of the critical need to move America forward again after it has moved backwards, we must unselfishly accept the personal responsibility to personally decrease in order to increase the probability of the success of a higher order. It is a success that will depend more upon our commitment and collaboration than on Obama who will face the unrealistic expectation of being able to simultaneously please everybody.

Barack Obama Critics Try to Discount His Overseas Success

Most of us are familiar with the fairy tale about the emperor who foolishly strutted around naked after being duped by a scam artist into believing he was wearing an invisible suit of clothes. The folly continued until a child spoke up and told the emperor the truth. Contrast that story with the one where Barack Obama went overseas and exceeded everyone's expectations and yet his critics expect the public to believe metaphorically that Obama "is not wearing any clothes." Will it take another child to dispel this nonsense?

Foreign policy was supposed to be John McCain's strong suit. In fact, this belief was so commonly accepted that McCain practically begged Obama to travel overseas. After all, Obama was "just an empty suit." Surely Obama would flounder on the world stage and then finally everyone would clearly see that McCain was better suited to lead the free world.

Does anyone have a mulligan lying around so that McCain can get a do-over? As other opponents have discovered the hard way, do not underestimate Obama. Like the Energizer Bunny, Obama just keeps going and going and going. After Obama's extraordinary reception on the world stage, the aimless wandering of the McCain campaign is destined to continue.

One hundred thousand people were expected to show up to hear Obama's speech in Germany. Instead, two hundred thousand people showed up, some even waved the American Flag. So what did the critics say? Take your pick. "I don't know how well it's going to play back in America with the great affection that Obama is receiving overseas." "Obama may be peaking too early... it's still a long ways to November." "Obama must be careful not to act too presidential." Then there is the ever popular slight that "Obama is just words." Surely that last one will stick since all of our previous presidents have campaigned as mimes.

Will the silliness ever cease? Instead of acting like professional wrestling promoters, is it too much to expect the media to admit that Obama is outperforming the competition? Obama is the smart kid who destroys the academic curve, the athlete who hits more homeruns or anyone who excels because of their special gift. It's a sad commentary that successful high potential people are commonly met with jealousy or attempts to discount their achievements.

Make no mistake about it; John McCain knows that his campaign is in trouble. In his dogfight against a <u>phenomenon</u> opponent, McCain thinks his only chance for victory is to get one of his nonsensical accusations about Obama to stick. His prospects are not good, because intelligent people would have to believe a charade that Barack Obama, the best option to lead America now, is not wearing any clothes.

CHAPTER 11 ~ August 2008

Joe Biden Will Be a Nightmare for John McCain and GOP

For months the GOP thought that Hillary Clinton would give them the most trouble as their 2008 Democratic presidential rival. That was before Barack Obama outperformed everyone's expectations and won the Democratic nomination. Suddenly, the GOP came to the realization that Obama was really the most formidable opponent and Hillary was the easier quarry. The Clinton dynasty was weakened and the GOP smelled red meat.
For strategic reasons, they wanted Hillary to stay in the mix. So they activated a plan to propel Hillary into the number two spot on the Democratic ticket. Why not? They could still run the same campaign ads produced months ago in anticipation of Clinton being the nominee.

In the meantime, they decided to follow <u>Karl Rove's</u> advice to redefine Obama and do a John McCain makeover. So the GOP further exploited the Clinton storyline of "Obama not appealing to working class white voters. Obama is elitist, Obama is weak on foreign policy and Obama makes great speeches, but they are only empty words." Attack, attack, attack. Poke your finger in Obama's chest and dare him to fight back in violation of his personal oath to run a civil campaign. Bait Obama to respond forcefully, because then you could proclaim that "He is no different than the rest of us."

However, true to form the GOP again miscalculated. They violated a basic tactic of war. Never back your opponent into a corner without giving them an escape route. Because with no way out, the trapped tend to fight back with more tenacity or call for backup. Barack Obama chose both options. As John McCain said, Obama became "testy", but he also placed a call to his colleague, Joe Biden, for backup. We know Joe Biden's reputation. He is salt of the earth, strong with working class Americans, strong with Catholics, strong with foreign policy and one who loves a good fight. And unlike Obama, Biden possesses no restriction to play nice. Biden has more than enough gut punches to go around and like Donna Brazile who tore into a GOP pundit, he won't hesitate to use them.

The GOP must be thinking they can't catch a cold. "Curses, foiled again!" "What's a body to do?" Maybe they will take the advice of the "brilliant" GOP talking head who recommended that McCain ignore Biden and keep hammering away at Obama. As in close your eyes and pretend that Biden isn't really there and just maybe he will go away. After witnessing Joe Biden in action, somehow I don't think that strategy will find much success.

The Longest Faces in the Room....

Tonight at the Democratic Convention, U.S. Senator Claire McCaskill was on point when she told MSNBC's Keith Olbermann that the longest faces in the room tonight belonged to the mainstream media who were disappointed that their promotion of Democratic Party disunity had lost its steam. She accurately proclaimed that Democrats are unified.

Also tonight, President Bill Clinton got his legacy back on track. He was outstanding with his talking points. Sen. John Kerry's speech which the egotistical media somehow didn't deem newsworthy was also outstanding. I watched it on C-Span.

Furthermore, it was no surprise that newsman Chuck Todd was way off target if he thought that we who were watching and listening at home would give a bucket of spit for his opinion that Sen. Joe Biden somehow flubbed his zingers. Joe Biden did just fine. All the speeches were impressive and inspiring when judged on content rather than some clueless critique by a reporter.

The Democrats will do just fine in November and then a President Barack Obama and his team will be as successful as were President Clinton and his team in returning our nation to prosperity.

Hillary Reconciled My Differences

As an early and <u>enthusiastic supporter</u> of Hillary Clinton, a schism developed between us during the contentious Democratic primary season. It was a split that I primarily blame on Hillary choosing to follow bad advice from her campaign advisers. However, tonight after listening to her speech at the Democratic Convention, my former irreconcilable differences have been reconciled. I also believe that Hillary has at last reconciled her disappointment in losing the Democratic nomination to Barack Obama. I hope that Hillary supporters are finally able to move forward and heartily support the Obama and Joe Biden Democratic ticket.

During her speech I saw the Hillary that I admired and felt was the Democrats best choice for president. But sometimes our best laid plans do not always materialize. Maybe for Hillary there is another calling. If she chooses, in Hillary I see someone that has the passion and drive to one day replace Ted Kennedy in the Senate as the lead and long term advocate for change that improves the lives of everyday working Americans. And that is no small consolation. The legacy of Ted Kennedy will be equal to that of any American President.

Barack Obama is the best choice at this time to be President of the United States. Americans really have tired of the gridlock in Washington and really have grown to despise consistent votes in Congress that strictly adhere to party lines at the detriment of the American people. Barack offers the best hope for moving beyond partisan politics. So I am encouraged that America will do the right thing in November and elect Barack Obama president. I'm also encouraged that Hillary Clinton and Bill Clinton will be partners to Barack and Joe Biden in helping America regain the prestige that it lost under the leadership of George Bush and Dick Cheney.

The "Real" Reason That John McCain Chose Sarah Palin

Anyone with an ounce of objectivity knows that Sarah Palin is not a good choice to serve as John McCain's vice president. McCain is 72 years old and suffers from skin cancer, a potentially deadly disease. So why pick an inexperienced running mate when there exist a tremendous need to assure the American public that a McCain Presidency has a good succession plan? The answer is right in front of us.

After watching the successful and unified Democratic Convention, John McCain knows that his candidacy is in trouble. However, McCain is also very proud. So short of admitting defeat, he picked an unqualified running mate so that after he loses; he has established an alibi that lets him save face. McCain wants to be able to rationalize that the American people did not reject him, but instead rejected his ticket because of legitimate concerns about the qualifications of Sarah Palin.

What McCain and the GOP have essentially done amounts to a punt. They are resigned to losing to Obama in 2008, then run interference during an Obama Presidency. Then try their chances again in 2012. If this was a blowout basketball game you would say that McCain has pulled his starters.

Now the real challenge for Team Obama and Biden is to stay focused and not reduce their game to the level of the competition. Like any disciplined team that wants to protect its lead, Team Obama and Biden should keep their full court press intact. Otherwise, Barack Obama and Joe Biden could end up adding their names to the long list of overly-confident teams that lost to a lesser opponent.

CHAPTER 12 ~ September 2008

The Mass Deception of McCain and Palin

The Republicans are tricky. When Tim Kaine was on the Democratic vice presidential short list, GOP strategist Karl Rove argued that Kaine's experience as a former mayor of Richmond, a small city, along with being Governor of Virginia, a state that actually has people residing in it, would not sufficiently be prepared to serve in the U.S. Presidency. Contrast Rove's assessment of the readiness of Gov. Kaine to his current assessment of Sarah Palin. Although Palin's experience includes being the former mayor of a small Alaskan village and as the current Governor of Alaska, the largest state in the nation but with a population smaller than a medium-sized American city, Rove claims that Palin is ready for the U. S. presidency. Republicans must think that the American people are stupid.

In grand forked-tongue fashion, the GOP plan of mass deception is in full gear. The plan calls for mocking Democratic successes which empirical data shows can be very effective. Just ask John Kerry. Of course any good GOP plan includes attacking the media to energizes their base. Their claim that the media is being extra hard on Palin is pure rubbish. After Alaska trooper-gate, and lies about selling an airplane on eBay for a profit, and five colleges in six years, someone had better take a microscopic look into Sarah Palin's background given that as vice president, Palin would be a heartbeat away from the presidency.

Nonetheless, credit the GOP credit for their cockiness. While accusing the media of gender bias, they have the audacity to try to bully Oprah Winfrey, another female, into featuring Sarah Palin as a guest on her television show. Yes, this is the same Sarah Palin that the GOP is trying to shield from press conferences and mainstream news shows such as Meet the Press. The GOP knows that Oprah like Hillary Clinton is as tough as nails and that Oprah will not blink. However, with my cynic on, I see the Oprah ploy as a veiled attempt by the GOP to inject race into the final weeks of the presidential campaign. And we all know that next to media-bashing, race-baiting is a GOP candidate-in-trouble strategy favorite.

Is McCain in trouble? If you swallow the Dr. Jekyll and Mr. Hyde polling data you might miss the fact that McCain is in trouble. When I listen to Rasmussen and Zogby analyze likely voter trends, it's clear to me that these guys are everything but objective. When they include sampling data from young voters who are part of the Obama movement, then I might place more stock into their opinions. To the chagrin of the GOP, I expect a majority of these young Obama supporters to show up on Election Day. That's when the GOP will see that despite their negative attempts to turn Obama's popularity against him, being a "celebrity" will be a bonus.

So Barack, Republicans do think that we are stupid. But this time I sense that enough people are tired of the same old politics which have a snowball chance in the hot place of undergoing any substantial overhaul in a government led by the same old McCain. Therefore Barack, I'm optimistic that after this election, media pundits will be scratching their heads trying to explain how the United States ended up on the right side of history, despite organized and determined efforts to preserve a culture of more of the same. I hope the pundits begin by proclaiming an end to a nation of red and blue states and hail the reemergence of the United States.

Obama Needs a Little Help from His Sisters

I have been taught that a gentleman never hits a lady. So what do you do when the lady fails to act like a lady? What do you do when the lady tells lies on you or keys your car or spits in your face or pokes you in the chest knowing that if you retaliate, you are the one who will get in trouble? I'll tell you what you do. You get help from your sister. Because while a sister may give you a hard time or pretend like she doesn't care, nothing will anger her quicker than when another woman tries to take advantage of her brother.

So while you attempt to retain the self-discipline that you were taught as a child and play nice, a sister will call or text that heifer (a word that your sister would use), and demand "that she stop messing with her brother." Yep, that's what your sister would do.

Barack Obama needs help right now from one or more of his sisters, because Sarah Palin is kicking him in the shin and it hurts. She is busily telling lies about Obama to any and everyone who will listen and when she self-embellishes, no one seems to care. Being true to his upbringing, Barack certainly can't gut-punch Palin, but there is nothing to prevent his sisters from coming to his rescue. So Caroline Kennedy, Kathleen Sebelius, Jennifer Granholm, Nancy Pelosi...please call or text Sarah and tell her to leave your brother alone...because if she doesn't, you will be waiting to have an up close sister to sister conversation with her at 3 p.m. when school lets out.

McCain vs. Obama Polls Forecast Trouble for GOP

Driven by Jerry Springer-like reporting from the mainstream media, current polling data of likely voter preferences show that the presidential contest between Barack Obama and John McCain is in a <u>dead heat</u>. On the surface, it may appear that the Obama Campaign has lost some momentum as a result of the media frenzy surrounding the selection of Sarah Palin as McCain's running mate. On the contrary, if you take a deeper look, you will find Obama still sitting in the catbird seat.

McCain with the addition of Palin has made a small dent into Obama's lead. McCain and his surrogates also have been playing the media to guarantee favorable reporting about Palin. At every turn the GOP has been yelled foul in order to provide cover for Palin who is neither ready for primetime nor ready to be a heartbeat away from the presidency. Nevertheless, the GOP strategy has found a measure of success, but there are signs that the media honeymoon for McCain and Palin is about to end.

The media has started to call McCain and his surrogates on the carpet for making a series of false and misleading statements about Obama and for routinely using questionable talking points that cast Palin in a more positive light. Compounding McCain's problems is the return of Obama from what some have felt was too passive a stay on the sidelines. Democrats cannot help but be encouraged that Obama appears refreshed and ready for hand-to-hand combat for the home stretch of the 2008 presidential contest. So at this point in the game, being even in a poll of likely voters is not reason for celebration for McCain.

Republicans are scared silly because they know that polling data that forecast a dead heat of likely voters, spells big trouble. In 2008, the historical voting preferences for "likely voters" do not include the millions of cellphone-toting, new and highly motivated Barack Obama supporters that are absolutely giddy with excitement as they await the opportunity to cast votes for Obama in numbers so astounding that political pundits will be left speechless.

So for anyone who thinks otherwise, the Obama phenomenon and movement are still running with a full tank. In fact the Obama tank is so full that McCain is attempting to siphon off Obama's idea of change. Imagine that? Since picking Palin as running mate, McCain now touts change as being more important than experience. Welcome aboard John, better late than never. However, your idea of change is not change that the American people can afford to believe in.

Pollsters and GOP Lack Walter Cronkite-Like Standard

A few days ago, I offered my opinion that any poll of likely voters is extremely unreliable for this 2008 Presidential Election. It appears that Dick Diver of the DailyKos agrees with my sentiments. According to Diver, the well-regarded Gallup Poll intentionally changed their polling methodology to favorably skew the bounce that John McCain got coming out of the GOP Convention. The poll of likely voters showed McCain with a 54-44 lead over Barack Obama. It's significant that McCain has a lead, because a poll of likely voters showing an even contest spells big trouble for the GOP. The polling data doesn't accurately predict voter preferences of new and Democratic-leaning voters that primarily use cellphones.

Embellishment of the facts has become standard operating procedure for the McCain Campaign. You know things are bad when conservatives take other conservatives to task as Andrew Sullivan recently did with Sarah Palin and as Karl Rove did with the McCain Campaign. Telling the truth is important again? It appears that the McCain and Palin honeymoon has officially ended. Now maybe we can talk about things that really matter such as how McCain helped invent the Blackberry. But seriously, where can we turn to get Walter Cronkite-like integrity?

Until recently, I thought the place to turn to was POTUS '08 on XM Radio. However, its claim of being "Politically neutral" was questionable this morning. As I listened to Scott Walterman, on the "The Morning Briefing", interview Susie Turnbull of the DNC, I was dismayed that Walterman tried to refute most of what Turnbull had to say about McCain. Turnbull talked about how McCain was making the claim that the U.S. economy was still strong despite the problems on Wall Street. Walterman acted like McCain's press secretary and awkwardly injected how polls showed that McCain was gaining in New Jersey and even managed to sarcastically remark how Obama would travel to Hollywood later in the day. "Unbiased." That depends on your definition of unbiased. Another listener who apparently heard the same interview, emailed Walterman, who in turn read it on the air, and offered their assessment of his conduct, "bag of hot air."

So a lesson to the wise, don't sweat the small stuff. Debatable polls numbers or "hot air" commentators are definitely small stuff. Seeing beyond the trees is probably not their objective. Don't allow them to drain your energy. Instead participate in the only poll that will really matter. Vote for change in November.

Rothschild McCain Endorsement Marks Return of Silly Season

Say it ain't so! Another sore loser gone wild? Barack Obama warned us that this was the silly season of politics. He also pointed out that Republicans must think that the American people are really stupid. Add to that list of people who think that we are really stupid, Republicans who masquerade as Democrats. After reading that former Hillary Clinton supporter, Lynn Forester de Rothschild, doesn't like Obama because she thinks that he is elitist, I had a compulsion to hear what other gobbly goop would emerge from her lips. So this afternoon I listened to Rothschild's press conference and wasn't surprised when she showered listeners with a generous portion of more nonsense as to the reason that she is endorsing John McCain.

Allow me to comment on some of Rothschild's more outrageous reasons for endorsing the McCain-Palin ticket. Maybe we should begin by telling Ms. Rothschild that with a name like Forester de Rothschild with residences in both the U.S. and England, maybe her assessment that Obama is elitist lacks credibility. Maybe she misspoke.

When Rothschild tried to discount Obama's contributions to ethics reform in the Senate, she blurted out that "Facts matter, Mr. Obama!" Hmmmm, facts matter, Mr. Obama. I guess Rothschild deliberately added "Mr. Obama" to the end of her statement because apparently she didn't want anyone to be confused with her seemingly contradictory feelings that "facts don't matter, Mr. McCain" or "facts don't matter, Mrs. Palin." The old double standard lives.

Something else I found amusing was Rothschild's assertion that Sen. Obama would be unduly influenced by Nancy Pelosi and Howard Dean and the centrist viewpoint would be non-existent. In fact she finds that prospect, "terrifying!" That's beyond interesting, that's perplexing. Terrified that the country would move too far to the left, but not terrified with the prospect of another Bush-like president in John McCain who showed questionable judgment with his selection of an enormously unqualified running mate to be a heartbeat away from the Presidency. Now as the saying goes, if that's not terrifying, then I don't know what terrifying is. And apparently neither does Ms. Rothschild.

Lastly, Ms. Rothschild "hopes her decision to publicly endorse McCain will give like-minded Democrats the confidence [or cover] to follow suit." First of all Ms.

Rothschild, you do not sound like a Democrat and there probably aren't a large number of silver spoon Democrats walking around in a like-mind that unlike you are immune to the negative effects of living under a failing economy run into the ground under the leadership of Republicans. Yep, there probably aren't a lot of like-minded Democrats who are oblivious to high gas prices, inadequate health care for their families, little money to send their kids to college or little income to help an aging parent. Good luck with your quest.

Yes Barack, it really is the silly season of politics, but because of the serious state of affairs, it is not a laughing matter. We do not need more Rothschild clones that are smarting from the defeat of their favorite candidate. We need more like-minded Americans committed to turning away from more of the same and possessing the wisdom to embrace your idea of <u>change that we can believe in</u>. I remain hopeful.

Telltale Signs That North Carolina Really Is In Play

North Carolina Democrats are excited about Barack Obama, their nominee for President of the United States. Volunteers are rapidly increasing in number and monetary contributions are flowing like the Nile River. Add to that the growing number of Obama/Biden bumper stickers and yard signs which unlike in previous years outpace those of GOP candidates. Extra telling is the comment sections of the editorial pages of leading NC newspapers like the Charlotte Observer where Obama supporters are active participants. Negative or distorted comments posted by GOP supporters or surrogates are quickly addressed and rebuffed.

Another very prominent sign that NC is in play is the attention being paid to NC by the Obama Campaign. Last Sunday Joe Biden and his wife Jill visited Charlotte. Michelle Obama visited on Thursday and Barack himself will be in Charlotte tomorrow on Sunday. Judging from the buzz that I hear, I expect the turnout for Obama to be huge. The turnout and the energy his appearance will generate will fire up supporters even more for the stretch run and attract the few voters left who still may be undecided.

If you need more proof, just listen to the chatter coming from the GOP and faux Democrats. Former Hillary Clinton supporter, Mark Erwin is quick to suggest that it is futile for Obama to expend resources in NC because it's not likely that the so-called solid red state will turn blue. It's obvious that much like his GOP pals; Erwin wasn't listening when Obama said "It's not red or blue states, but the United States." Also, he apparently discounted a recent poll of likely NC voters that showed John McCain with only a one point lead over Obama. That will spell big trouble for the GOP, because of the revised composition of likely voters that include a three to one Democratic advantage of new registrants and a large number of difficult to canvass young voters that favor Barack Obama. Indeed, NC is very much in play.

Still not convinced? Prominent GOP candidates like Pat McCrory who is running for governor and Libby Dole up for re-election to the U.S. Senate seem to be running as Independents. Libby Dole didn't even attend the GOP Convention. Who's a Republican? There is little mention of John McCain and with her star now losing its luster; few are climbing on the Sarah Palin bandwagon. Privately Republicans must be furious with McCain that Palin was not properly vetted. With almost a scandal a day, voters have to be questioning the judgment and decision-making capacity of McCain over his choice of Palin. The selection of Joe Biden by Obama was a no-brainer. Does anyone really believe that McCain put country first with his selection of Palin to be a heartbeat away from becoming Commander in Chief?

Well, those examples validate NC as a battleground state, but the biggest indicator is it appears that most NC voters are not of the stupid variety and have discerned that the country desperately needs positive change. I have attended large and small Obama events and there is widespread support for Obama from the electorate. Those supposedly white, bitter, disenfranchised voters don't live here. You may recall it was Obama's NC primary victory that helped him get his mojo back. Much like it is with Iowa, NC and Obama are now joined at the hip. So despite this being the silly season of politics, Obama has statewide support in the Coastal Plains, the Piedmont and the Mountain regions of the Old North State. Yes, telltale signs suggest that the debilitating American Gridlock will get a long overdue positive change injection on November 4 and NC most certainly will line up on the right side of history.

Obama Makes Blue Gains, McCain Seeks to Redshirt His Campaign

John McCain is still in trouble when the polls show the presidential contest even. Now when the latest Washington Post national poll shows Barack Obama turning the country Democratic blue with his nine-point lead over McCain, it's panic time. McCain and his advisers are in disarray and desperately seek to stem the tide by any means necessary. Their initial response was to refute the polling data as bogus, but that is tame compared to what McCain and his advisers are now trying to accomplish. Fully realizing the necessity to stop the Obama surge before it's too late; McCain has announced the suspension of his presidential campaign. He has taken this unprecedented action supposedly to focus full attention on the current economic crisis. In addition, McCain wants to postpone his Friday debate with Obama.

To use a sports analogy, athletes often seek a postponement or red-shirt from competition when they lack adequate preparation. Therefore, I suspect the unspoken reason that McCain is seeking a postponement is because he feels unprepared to face Obama in a debate on Friday. In essence, McCain wants red-shirt status in the homestretch of a presidential contest to avoid falling further behind in the polls.

It wouldn't surprise me if McCain also tried to delay the presidential election...until he is ready. For someone who brags about being ready to assume the presidency on Day One, McCain is not even ready to debate his opponent on Day One. As more Americans turn their attention to the serious business of electing the next president, when they objectively assess the qualifications of McCain and Obama, McCain will be rejected as unacceptable. No longer a straight talker, McCain seemed to have lost his way. He is running a typical slash and burn GOP campaign strategy overflowing with personal attacks, innuendos and flat out lies about Obama. Dishonesty reigns.

Even today when Obama reached out to McCain with an offer to tackle the economic crisis in a nonpartisan manner, McCain shamelessly tried to take advantage of Obama's gesture by claiming to be its originator. What a peculiar way to build trust and lay a foundation for reaching across the aisle. That kind of behavior will ensure a continuation of Washington gridlock. Nevertheless, the game continues. No one knows when McCain will unveil his next brilliant idea. However, if his un-presidential attempt to red-shirt is any indication, no one but McCain's most fanatical supporters expect his idea to be anything remotely worthwhile.

Unprepared McCain Ducks and Runs from Competition

We have heard all too often that John McCain is a great war hero. Granted. But when our war hero was presented with his latest opportunity to show his bravery, he ducked and ran from of all things a debate against Barack Obama that would require him to answer some tough questions about the <u>economy</u>. When America badly wants to hear from McCain and Obama, to say that McCain is running scare would be an understatement.

Maybe someone should tell McCain that it's hard to lead from the rear. The debate is tomorrow night and the State of Mississippi has invested a lot of time and money in the preparation of the debate site. Obama recognizes that the President must multi-task even when the going gets tough and he <u>still plans to show up for the debate</u> with or without McCain. Someone should tell McCain that if he fails to reverse his dumb political stunt, the beating that he is receiving now in the polls will pale in comparison to the whipping he will endure after tomorrow night.

At no time in recent history has America needed leadership as much as it needs it right now with the country being threatened with financial collapse and war still raging in Iraq. McCain had a golden opportunity to show Americans that he was ready to lead, but instead disengaged from a hotly contested presidential race against Obama. Americans are left scratching their heads like they were when McCain showed another lapse in judgment with his selection of <u>dangerously unprepared Sarah Palin</u> as his running mate. Presidential decision making capacity...it's debatable.

CHAPTER 13 ~ October 2008

Decision 2008: Obama/Biden to DC, McCain/Palin to Hollywood

It's becoming more and more apparent that the majority of Americans have decided to go to the polls and send Barack Obama and Joe Biden to the White House. However, John McCain and Sarah Palin can take solace in knowing that they both have bright futures in Hollywood. When I listened to McCain's stand-up routine at the Alfred E. Smith Dinner in New York, I found him to be extremely funny. And McCain's Michael Jordan-like tongue wagging episode after the last Presidential Debate with Obama, surely will one day rank with the now infamous Howard Dean scream. Fred Thompson, be on notice. You have new competition.

Not to be outdone, Sarah Palin's performance during the lone Vice-Presidential Debate showed that she has actress-like skills in memorizing a script. She could make millions in Hollywood if she chose to go that route full-time and eventually she could even win an Oscar. You betcha. Palin does Palin much better than Tina Fey and Palin's upcoming appearance on SNL should be a real hoot.

So it's a win-win situation for all. Obama and Biden can tackle the serious issues the country faces while McCain and Palin fans can follow their act to Hollywood. It's refreshing to see that most Americans finally realize that it's more important to the sustainability of America to have a President and Vice President with the intellect to tackle major issues than average Joes we feel comfortable having a beer with at the local pub. It's worth noting that Obama/Biden supporters must validate their wisdom by actually casting their votes.

A NC Wish for a Palin-Only Ticket and Signs of an Obama Victory

The North Carolina GOP is a disillusioned mess. NC Republicans and some faux Democrats are surely depressed about the waning prospect that North Carolina will remain in the GOP column in 2008. And disregard that Rasmussen Poll nonsense showing John McCain with a two-point lead. North Carolina voters prefer Barack Obama and the telltale signs are still in place. And the signs are growing. In rush hour traffic on Friday, I was shocked (yet amused) to see that the McCain/Palin bumper sticker on the truck in front of me...was minus the McCain. The driver showed outright contempt for McCain by displaying only "Palin." A sign of the times? Maybe. McCain may be wise to spend less time running negative Obama ads and spend more time reining in fellow Republicans who are starting to abandon his sinking ship.

Jesse Helms wouldn't recognize this North Carolina. While McCain slept, Obama quietly surrounded the fort. It's been a long time since any Democratic presidential candidate has enjoyed the kind of widespread support that Obama now has in North Carolina. But don't expect any Obama premature victory lap. The Obama Campaign is not taking North Carolina for granted. With the Obama Campaign "fight until the last vote is counted strategy", I predict that Obama will win North Carolina in a manner reminiscent of the way that Usain Bolt won his Olympic medals. And the Obama victory will have coattails.

Kay Hagan is almost certain to unseat Libby Dole, the North Carolina Senator from Kansas, and Bev Perdue will win a closely contested governor's race and defeat Pat McCrory who is giving her a run for her money. Give McCrory, the Charlotte mayor, credit for being smart enough not to alienate Obama supporters with whom he hopes to garner some measure of favor. All in all, it's been a great year to follow North Carolina politics. And the person most responsible is Barack Obama. It is satisfying to witness that most Americans including North Carolinians see the value of having a leader that possesses the ability to inspire people to transform a nation.

CHAPTER 14 ~ November 2008

Mavericks Need Not Apply...We Need Change Agents

Joe Biden was right. "John McCain really doesn't get it". At a time when the American people have loudly spoken and asked for real change, McCain is still running around foolishly touting his maverick credentials. Well let me tell you what a maverick does. A maverick defines the United States in terms of red states and blue states. A maverick preserves a doctrine of Conservatives against Liberals, Republicans versus Democrats. A maverick doesn't seek change, but wants more of the same. A maverick guarantees the continuation of political gridlock.

Just like the lead characters Bret and Bart Maverick who were nomad gamblers in the old TV western Maverick, McCain has no real plan but runs from place to place in search of a good poker hand or campaign slogan that will stick. And like Bret and Bart who regularly threw their chips up to see where they would land, the maverick McCain abruptly threw his hands up in the midst of a crisis as in "I am suspending my campaign and returning to Washington."

So I don't think the country needs a maverick or a reformer who wants to put a band aid on a gaping wound, but it needs a change agent like Barack Obama who knows that if we keep doing things the same old way we're going to get the same old results. Well Joe, while John McCain doesn't get it, the early voting results tells me that the American people get it. That's true here in the great state of North Carolina, where this time around, North Carolina refuses to stay a maverick red state, but looks forward to rejoining the United States.

Sometimes a Burden Goes Undetected...Until It's Removed

The Wizard of Oz is one of my favorite movies. It is filled with many transformations. One of the most memorable ones is the scene where the house falls on the wicked witch of the west. The black and white movie transformed into color and instantly everything became brighter. That's the feeling I got when Barack Obama was declared President-Elect. Instantly everything became brighter. And when Barack spoke to the people, tears flowed like the Nile River.

They were tears of joy and tears of disbelief. Like most Black people in America and apparently a lot of White people too, I never thought that in my lifetime, I would see a Black man elected President of the United States. I know that the country talks a good game when it comes to equal rights, but on this night, actions spoke louder than words. I felt a burden lifted from my shoulders that quite frankly I didn't know existed. Something magical happened. It was a transformational moment.

It was as if for the first time in the history of America, Black people had obtained full citizenship. The reality was overwhelming. Jesse Jackson cried. Colin Powell cried. Condoleezza Rice cried. Oprah Winfrey cried. Even Barack Obama's Fox News nemesis, Juan Williams, cried. All accomplished Americans; they too were overcome by emotions that refused to wait for a private moment. And it wasn't just Black people that experienced that Twilight Zone feeling. I saw that same look of disbelief in the faces of White Americans as well. And they also were not immune to emotional release. Stephen Colbert on Comedy Central cried and White commentators interviewing crying Black people, cried as well.

Barack Obama had said that now was our time for change. He had inspired us with his words and now was chosen to lead us. And John McCain was so gracious in defeat. Even though Obama was not the unanimous choice of White Americans, it doesn't matter. No longer can it be said that America will not elect a Black person as president. Black Americans now look at White Americans differently and there is absolutely nothing that they can do about it. There is a feeling of greater trust. And the so-called great divide between Black and Hispanic Americans is now formally declared a myth. A transformational event has taken place and a burden that many of us didn't realize existed, has been lifted.

CHAPTER 15 ~ January 2009

Barack Obama is a President of the People

President Barack Obama exudes confidence and it is contagious. He is quickly becoming the president of the people. Americans are really excited about the positive energy that he is generating and despite hard times, people are optimistic about the future. President Obama faces high expectations. However, with a smile on his face, the President has said that he is eager to get started in his quest to get the country and yes even the world back on the right track. And it appears that the people are committed to helping.

Some critics will try to focus on little things when trying to define the success of the Obama presidency. But Obama represents an American success. He is already on the mountaintop and America sits there with him. There are no more blue or red states or liberals or conservatives or special interests. Instead, President Obama is leading the charge for a United States of America much as he communicated during his presidential campaign. He wants a country where it's okay to disagree but advocates doing so without being disagreeable.

That's why it's okay to have Rev. Rick Warren pray at his inauguration and that's why it's okay for the good reverend to invoke the name of Jesus. We don't all have to be on the same page or walk in lockstep or risk being dismissed as not relevant. That's the old way. The election of Barack Obama was the beginning of a new way and the movement which he is leading now has wheels. Persons like Rush Limbaugh who is slow to accept this fact that change has come to America will have a tough period of adjustment.

Rush does not stand alone as an obstacle to a better America. He has teammates, because many who perceive change as a loss of power or influence will stand with him. So President Obama shouldn't be surprised when he encounters resistance from the so-called political Right and the Left, Republicans and Democrats, White and <u>Black</u> Americans, the <u>media</u>, and countless others who will insist on skinning their cats the same way. However, the countless followers, who have heeded the call to help President Obama make positive change a <u>group effort</u> and a reality, appear to have the upper hand.

EPILOGUE

President Obama has become President of the United States during one of the worse periods in its history. Despite the hard economic conditions being experienced by many Americans, some Republicans are boldly asserting that they want President Obama to fail. It's amazing that before the new president was in office for a month, GOP hopefuls were jockeying for their party's 2012 presidential nomination. With selfish disregard for the well being of the United States, these GOP hopefuls will guarantee that the American people will support and empower President Obama in his effort to help restore America's credibility in the world.

In the meantime, whether President Obama succeeds of fails, change has come to America. There are those who consider Obama's election as the fulfillment of Dr. Martin Luther King's dream. I wouldn't go quite that far, but Obama's election does represent major progress in race relations in this country. Black parents can now tell their children with confidence that they can grow up and become president of the United States. Regardless of the mind-set of the unconvinced cynic who argues otherwise, that point is indisputable. Furthermore, it's a historic milestone worthy of commemoration.

ABOUT THE AUTHOR

Steveson Terrell was born and raised in North Carolina. He is a self-described eternal optimist. A graduate of North Carolina A&T State University with a degree in business administration, Steveson has served in leadership roles in both the public and private sectors. In addition, he has been an adjunct lecturer and served his country in the United States Military. Steveson professes to have a lifelong passion for politics and social justice and keeps life in perspective by neither taking himself or others too seriously.

www.ingramcontent.com/pod-product-compliance
Lightning Source LLC
Chambersburg PA
CBHW060631290526
45793CB00001B/215